MARY WITHALL spent thirty five years in Secondary and Further Education, lecturing in Natural Sciences, Nutrition and Health subjects before retiring to the Island of Easdale in Argyll in 1988. She became the archivist to the Easdale Island Museum in 1989 and has been associated with the museum ever since. She is a founder member and trustee of the Slate Islands Heritage Trust which was formed in March 2000.

In 1995 Mary published the first of her trilogy of historical novels based on the history of the Slate Islands: *Beacon on the Shore, The Gorse in Bloom* and *Where the Wild Thyme Grows* (published by Hodder & Stoughton in paperback at £5.99.) Since then she has published three further novels all of which are available in paperback.

D0550252

All royalties generated from sales of this book go to the
Slate Islands Heritage Trust.

Easdale, Belnahua, Luing & Seil:

The Islands That Roofed the World

MARY WITHALL

Luath Press Limited

EDINBURGH

www.luath.co.uk

First Edition 2001

The paper used in this book is acid-free, neutral-sized and recyclable.
It is made from low chlorine pulps produced in a low-energy, low
emission manner from renewable forests.

Printed and bound by
Bell & Bain Ltd., Glasgow

Typeset in 10.5 point Sabon by
S. Fairgrieve, Edinburgh, 0131 658 1763

Contents

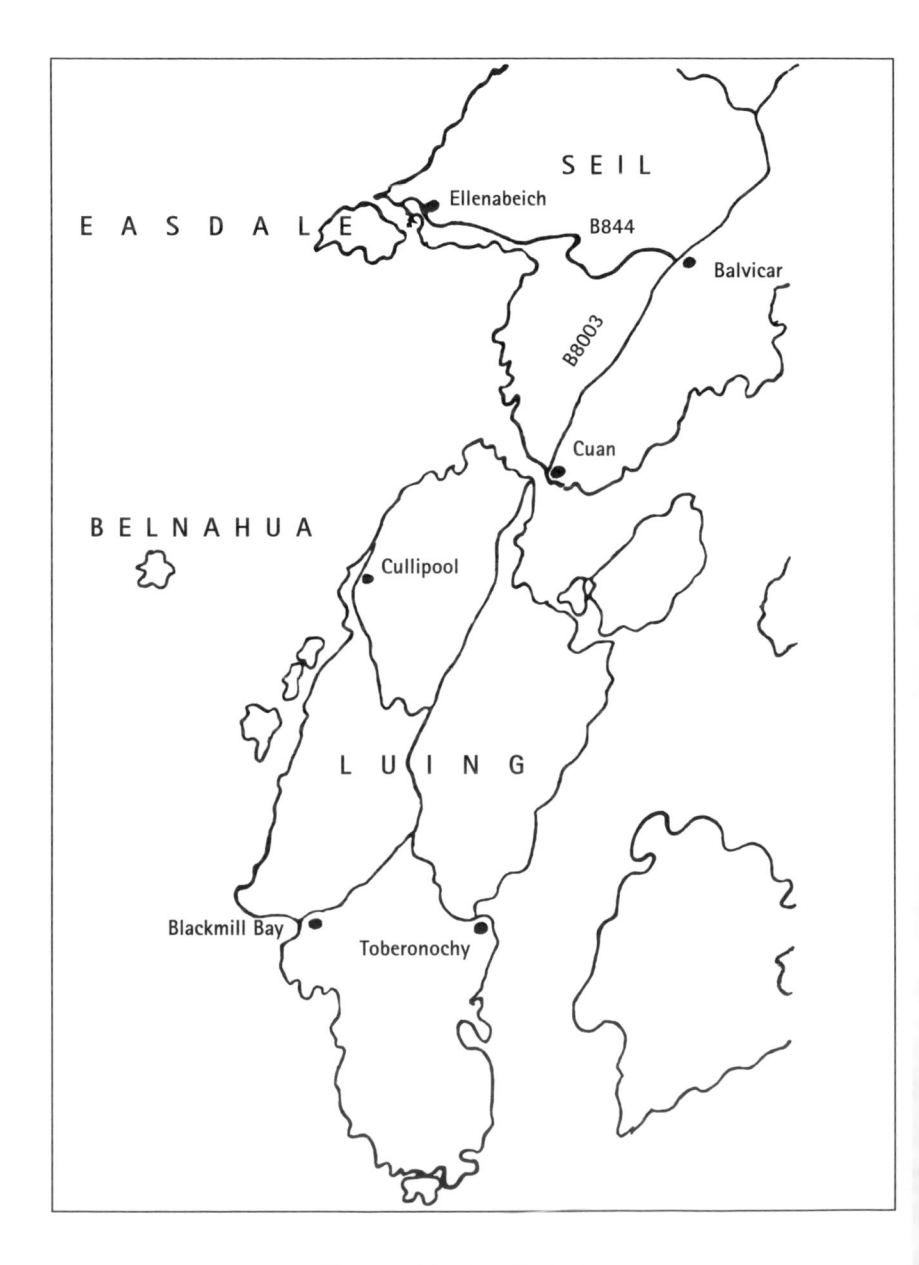

The Slate Islands of Netherlorn

Introduction

OFF THE WEST COAST of Argyll in the Sound of Lorn, a few miles South of Oban, lie the Slate Islands of Seil, Luing, Belnahua and Easdale. Easdale is less than a mile across in any direction, but is so rich in deposits of slate rock that it became the centre of one of the most important of Scotland's industries during the 18th and 19th centuries and gave its name to a band of geological strata stretching in a NE to SW direction right across the Highlands ... the Easdale Slate Belt.

From earliest recorded history slate was taken from the shores of Easdale Island. Large slabs of the rock were used to cover buildings and as grave- and hearthstones. Perhaps the Vikings landed here and carried away the slate to their various settlements along the coast. The first recorded account of Easdale slate is in the writings of Dean Munro circa 1554. Describing the islands of Lorn, Seill, Seunay and Lunge (probably Luing) he mentions under

Easdale Island

the heading, *Sklaitt, the litle iyle callit in Erische Leid Ellan Sklaitt, quherein ther is abundance of skalzie(slate) to be win.* This has been accepted by later historians as referring to Easdale.

As time went on, men learned to split the laminated rock into thinner and thinner sheets which could then be further divided into roofing slates as we know them today: rectangular pieces of rock which, when laid overlapping one another, form a watertight roof covering.

Many ancient and prestigious buildings in Scotland are roofed with Easdale slate, Ardmaddy Castle in Lorn built in 1676, Stalker Castle in Appin built in 1631, Cawdor Castle in Invernesshire and Glasgow Cathedral both dating from the fourteenth century, among them.

The Slate Islands were part of an enormous tract of land twenty miles wide and stretching from Taymouth in the East to the coast of Argyll which formed the estate of the Breadalbane family, cousins of the Dukes of Argyll. By expeditious marriages and an uncanny knack of always being on the right side at the right time, the Breadalbane Campbells acquired this land and held it for more than four hundred years.

Naturally enough the Breadalbanes exploited the mineral resources of their own land so that we find many of the buildings they owned are roofed in Easdale slate, and since from the 18th century onwards, the title Marquis of Breadalbane carried with it the ownership of Nova Scotia, it is not surprising to discover public buildings in Eastern Canada which also bear roofs of Easdale slate. In the middle years of the 19th century, between 7 million and 19 million roofing slates were exported annually as far afield as New Zealand, Australia, the West Indies and the Eastern Seaboard of the United States of America, giving rise to the claim at that time that Easdale was roofing the world!

The Breadalbane estates were broken up early in the 20th century and the productive land was sold off in parcels mainly for agricultural purposes. Seil and Luing were split up into a few privately owned farms, while the village properties were sold off to indivudual home-owners. Belnahua, abandoned early in the

20th century, has remained uninhabited, the island's owner living on Luing. Easdale Island, having little to offer a developer other than slate, which following the First World War became an uneconomic commodity, remained unsold until the 1950s when it was purchased by a local man, Donald Dewer. Under his ownership the island lay fallow, the only inhabitants being a very small population of elderly folk, the remnants of the once great slate quarrying industry. Subsequently the island has been owned by a succession of entrepreneurs each of whom has made some contribution to the island's economy and population growth. One of these gentlemen, Chris Nicholson, was responsible for the inauguration in 1981 of the Easdale Island Folk Museum which exhibits a fine collection of 19th century photographs and artefacts, is a source of genealogical information for descendants of the quarry workers and is the focal point for those wishing to explore and understand the remnants of the slate industry on the island.

In celebration of the new millennium, a group of local enthusiasts has come together to form the Scottish Slate Islands Heritage Trust whose aims are to identify, record, and wherever possible, preserve locations, buildings and artefacts relating to the Scottish Slate Industry and the social history of the islanders. The Trust's first major project was the inauguration, in the year 2000, of the Slate Islands Heritage Centre in Ellenabeich village on the Isle of Seil. All royalties from the sale of this book will be donated to the work of the Trust.

People visit the Slate Islands today for a variety of reasons. Perhaps they are intrigued by the notion that anyone would wish to live on this bleak and rugged coastline, bordering the wild Atlantic Ocean and often in locations accessible only by sea. Maybe they have heard of the slate industry and are genuine seekers after knowledge about Scotland's industrial past. Some are descendants of the hundreds of sturdy characters who lived and worked on the islands until such time as economic pressures caused the quarries to close and forced the men to seek a life elsewhere.

For whatever reason visitors arrive in the district, they cannot fail to be affected by the unique ambience of the different villages. The population of Easdale Island, for example, is moving into the 21st century while living in a village without cars, footpaths, streets or street lighting.

Easdale today

Visitors are never disappointed by the splendid panorama of sea and islands which can be viewed from the top of Smiddy Brae, nor, when roving in the wild places, can they pass without notice the thickets of grasses and wild flowers which in the course of the past century have endeavoured to heal the scars that Man's industry has left upon this glorious landscape.

Despite the noise, dust and general chaos created by the operation of an important industry, those who inhabited the Slate Islands a hundred years ago, while the quarries were in operation, were themselves moved by the beauty of their surroundings. Typical of their response is this sonnet, printed in the *Oban Times* of 25 March 1899, of which the author is identified only by his initials:

Thou Easdale, swept by storms and lashed by foam
Of angry seas, thy memory will last
In all its freshness whereso'ere be cast
My lot in life. Tho' far from thee I roam
My thoughts are still with thee; no spire or dome
Of mighty city can like thee hold fast
My thoughts; beside thy rocky shores were passed
The happy peaceful days; thou art my home.
The islets gird thee round, and far and nigh
Their rugged forms show clear against the sky;
In calm and sunshine nought can equal thee
But when the winds blow and the waves dash high
In grandeur, like a giant, strong and free
Thou stands't defiant in thy majesty.   E.A.R.W.

The stencil used by Easdale Slate Quarrying Co., 1860s

CHAPTER I

The Geology of the Slate Islands

THE BEDROCK OF THE district consists of some of the oldest sedimentary rock exposed in the British Isles. 650 million years ago during the Dalradian Period, two major land masses formed the area now known as Scotland. The mountains and plains of ancient Caledonia were bounded on their southern borders by a shallow sea occupying the area which lies between the Great Glen Fault and the Highland Boundary Fault. The area of this sea included Argyll and the Inner Hebridean Islands of Islay, Jura, Scarba and the islands in the Sound of Lorn. The second landmass covered the area of the Southern Uplands and the Border Country.

In the absence of vegetation and with great extremes of temperature the rock was rapidly broken down into boulders and stones small enough to be carried away by the fast flowing waters shed by the hills. Particulate material, breaking continuously into finer and finer particles as it travelled, was eventually deposited as silt and mud on the bed of the shallow sea.

Approximately 440 million years ago during the Ordovician period, extensive land movements took place during which great folding of the shallow sea deposits occurred. The concertina effect

Map of **EASDALE SLATE BELT** with inset map showing

outcrops near Oban

of this folding created enormous pressure in the layers of mud, compressing and heating the deposits until they were converted into slate rock, hornblende biotite schists and marble.

Easdale Slate is blue-black in colour, bears a ripple on its surface which distinguishes it from other smoother slates from Wales and Cornwall and is identified by the large quantity of iron pyrites it contains. This occurs as cubic crystals of what is often referred to as Fool's Gold. The crystals may be anything up to 15mm across and can be easily seen glistening on the wet slate roofs. They rarely rust and add an extra dimension to the attractive appearance of the slate.

The hornblend biotite schists occur in just a few places on the coast of Seil Island, along the northern edge of Shuna and penetrating in a NE-SW direction, the NE corner of Luing. Deposits of lead and even gold have been found in this rock but never in economically viable quantities.

Marble occurring in one spot only near Ardmaddy Castle was found to be of poor quality and although a quarry was opened up in 1745 to exploit it, it was quickly abandoned.

During the folding of the slate beds they were tipped over to an angle of between forty-five and forty-seven degrees. The dip of the rocks is clearly seen where slate is exposed in the now abandoned quarries and along the shore of Easdale. Post Dalradian, a long period of denudation resulted in a flat plain being formed across the upended slate beds. Over this, from time to time, there flowed laval outpourings of an andestic and basaltic nature. The rock so formed caps the slate beds and constitutes all the highest ground on the islands, including Dun Mor and the two parallel ridges bisecting Luing.

55 million years ago during the Tertiary Period, extensive volcanic activity centred on the Isle of Mull and resulted in the intrusion of a series of dykes and sills of molten lava which forced their way upwards through the existing strata. The Easdale Slate Beds were at this time crossed in a NW to SE direction by a series of large dykes and hundreds of smaller dykes and sills of Dolerite, a hard basaltic granite known locally as whinstone. Where the

Exposed slate

intrusions occur, the slate is deformed and crystallisation of minerals has occurred. There are often veins of quartz and greater concentrations of iron pyrites crystals at the junction of slate and Dolerite. At these sites the slate was not worth cutting out and the quarrymen described such areas as bad rock leaving them undisturbed. This accounts for the often jagged outlines of rock surfaces produced by weathering and for the uneven cutting of those quarries, now flooded, where buttresses and platforms can be observed at great depths through the water on a calm day. As a result of the denudation of softer rocks, volcanic plugs of whinstone can be seen about the district sticking up like so many upturned flowerpots.

The whinstone was used liberally as a building material on the islands, forming many of the cornerstones of the cottages and the industrial buildings. The early masons must have been particularly skilful in cutting and shaping this rock for even when using modern cutting and drilling equipment it is a difficult material to work.

Easdale 'cats'

Today the builder's worst nightmare is to encounter a 'whin dyke' while digging out the foundations of a house or excavating for a septic tank!

Along the shores rounded pebbles and larger stones may be found in abundance. These are of many different rock types and often bear no relation to the bedrock of the island. These sea-rounded stones are thought to represent glacial moraines carried South Westwards along the Great Glen Fault during the various Ice Ages. Jean Adams, one of Easdale's several artists in residence, has for many years painted lifelike images of cats on these stones. Some of our visitors return year after year to add to their family of Easdale cats.

CHAPTER 2

The Slate Industry
and the Breadalbanes

THE OWNER OF THE immense Breadalbane estates during the mid-18th century was John Campbell, Earl of Breadalbane. Together with three of his clansmen, Charles Campbell of Lochaline, Colin Campbell of Carwin and John Campbell, Cashier of the Royal Bank of Scotland, the Earl set up the Marble and Slate Quarrying Company of Netherlorn in 1745. While the remainder of Scotland was concerned with either assisting or preventing the accession of Prince Charles Edward Stuart to the throne, the Breadalbanes were taken up with matters more closely related to their pockets. It was this failure to take any side in the uprising which left the Breadalbane family still in possession of its vast wealth when other Highland chieftains had been impoverished, their lands confiscated by the Crown.

Prior to the formation of the Marble and Slate Company of Netherlorn, the Easdale slate deposits had for some time been exploited on a commercial basis by Colin Campbell of Carwin. From 1744 records exist of slates being taken from the Easdale quarry, so there were existing assets to be transferred to the Marble and Slate Company. According to the Minute Book held in the Scottish Records Office, the items sold included:

600,000 slates @ 16/8 [83p] per thousand = £550.8s.4d [£550.42]
7 sets of quarrying tools @ 17/10 [89p] = £6.4s.10d [£6.24]

Each set of tools consisted of the following items:

1 Big mallet	*2 or 3 dozen jumpers [large chisels]*
1 Lesser do.	*1 Driller*
1 Big Gavlock	*2 or 3 dozen wages [wedges] of various sizes*
1 Lesser do.	*4 Picks*
1 Small hammer	*2 Spades*
1 Slate knife	*1 Shovel*

The final sum paid by the Marble and Slate Company of Netherlorn when they completed the purchase of the Easdale quarries from Colin Campbell of Carwin in 1746, was £826.18s.8d [£826.93].

In the year 1745, when the Company took over from Carwin, more than a million slates had been manufactured. With the introduction of more workmen, better methods for cutting out the slate and engines for pumping the quarries dry, production rapidly increased. When Pennant visited Easdale in 1772, he was able to report that two and a half million slates were being exported from the island annually.

> Visited Easdale, the noted slate island: whose length is about half a mile and composed entirely of slate intersected and in some places covered with whin-stone to a thickness of sixteen feet; the stratum of slate is thirty six degrees, dipping quick SE to NW. In order to be raised it is first blasted with powder; the greater pieces are then divided, carried off in a wheel-barrow, and lastly split into merchantable sizes and put on board at the price of twenty shillings per thousand. About two millions and a half are sold annually to England, Norway, Canada and the West Indies.

The marble in the original title of the enterprise refers to an exposure of this rock in a small quarry close to Ardmaddy Castle, at that time the country residence of the Marquis. The marble proved to be too flawed for commercial use, and only one fireplace, in Ardmaddy Castle itself, is attributed to this source.

By the year 1800 production of roofing slates had risen to five million. This increase was due largely to the introduction of improved pumping machinery which made it possible to quarry the slate below sea level even at high tide. One quarry at Ellenabeich eventually reached a depth of 80 metres. The waste slate from here was used to form a causeway to the mainland which provided the foundations of the rows of cottages on the Seil side of Easdale Sound. Further quarries were opened at Cullipool, Maryport and Toberonochy on Luing and latterly, at Balvicar.

John, Second Marquis of Breadalbane, dissatisfied with the activities of the Marble and Slate Company of Netherlorn, bought out his co-directors in 1842 and took over the working of the Easdale quarries himself. With the assistance of an ingenious engineer, John Whyte, he introduced many examples of new technology of the day. Railway track was laid to assist transport of slates, a succession of gin engines (operated by horse power), and finally some of the most up to date steam pumps in use by the Royal Navy were installed in quarries which had earlier been declared redundant because they could no longer be pumped dry. Inclined planes were constructed in several of the quarries to facilitate hauling the slate to the surface and allowing the men themselves easier access to the workfaces, now as much as 70-80 metres below sea level.

Although he took an close interest in the mining and engineering activities taking place throughout his great estates, John Campbell appears to have had a particular liking for the Slate Islands and their people. He ordered improvements to the workmen's cottages as well as introducing railway tracks to carry the slate from the quarries to the various harbours. Together with his inventive and tireless manager, John Whyte, he relieved the people of much of the drudgery of their lives. Releasing the women and children from the task of carrying the slates on their backs meant that the women could spend more time caring for their families and the children could go to school, until the boys were old enough to work in the quarries and the girls could be sent out into service. It was the second Marquis who provided schooling for the quarrymen's children and evening classes for young boys once they had started work in the quarries. He appointed a medical officer, Hugh Gillies, to take care of the men and their families, and a system of medical insurance was introduced which meant that for a few shillings a year everyone received medical attention when they needed it.

John Campbell's country seat was Ardmaddy Castle, situated on the mainland only a mile or so from the Clachan Bridge which spans the Atlantic, the only road access to the Isle of Seil.

Standing upon a dome-shaped grassy mound, sheltered on three sides by tree-covered heights, Ardmaddy commands a view to the SW of outstanding beauty, a combination of sea, shoreline, wooded slopes and in the distance the whole panorama of the isles of Seil, Luing, Jura and Scarba. The present building was reconstructed and greatly extended in the late 18th century but the foundations date from the 15th century, when the marriage of Muriel of Calder and Sir John Campbell, second son of the Duke of Argyll, linked two great families and their vast estates. The union provided the Clan Campbell with enormous political weight together with excessive wealth, both of which were to endure into the first three decades of the 20th century.

On the death of John, the 5th Earl (2nd Marquis) of Breadalbane, in 1862, his successors preferred to occupy the family seat, Taymouth Castle, and Ardmaddy became merely a summer retreat. For much of the year it was occupied and maintained by His Lordship's Factor for the area.

In the early 1930s, when much of the Breadalbane fortune had been swallowed up by one economic crisis after another, and much of the estate had been parcelled up and sold off, the then Earl vacated the Breadalbane's great mansion, Taymouth Castle, and in fulfilment of an ancient prophecy, rode out of the valley on a white horse, carrying with him everything he possessed in the world.

From the earliest days slate had been shipped from Easdale to supply the burgeoning cities in the East, the Clyde Valley and the Borders. According to Pennant, as early as 1772, slate was also exported to England, Nova Scotia, the West Indies and Norway. By the 1860s, in addition to this long standing trade, regular exports were being made to eastern USA, New Zealand and Australia. Seven million slates left Easdale harbour bound for the colonies in 1862, the year in which John Campbell, Second Marquis of Breadalbane, died.

After John's death, the quarries continued to operate under the leadership of John Whyte while lawyers wrangled over the identity of the legitimate successor to the second Marquis. The Breadalbanes were singularly unsuccessful in producing male heirs and rarely did the title pass directly from father to son. So prolific were the Campbells however, that there was inevitably more than one claimant to the title.

In 1866, the various quarries at Easdale, Balvicar and those on Luing, at Cullipool and Toberonochy, were leased out and came under separate management. Commercial quarrying possibly began on Belnahua at about this period, the island being the only one of the group not owned by the Breadalbanes.

The quarries at Ellenabeich and on Easdale Island were leased to a consortium of businessmen from Glasgow, Messrs Andrew and Alexander Ross, Mr Hodge and Mr Dairy together with Mr J Gillespie, Slate Merchant of Paisley. For the first ten years the new Easdale Slate Quarrying Company prospered, living off the fat of earlier investment in machinery and equipment. As time went on, the operation became less efficient owing to a lack of any new investment and working conditions grew increasingly dangerous. The Quarry Manager, Mr McColl, bore the whole burden of the operation at this time and without the financial backing of his masters, he was powerless to improve the situation.

Following a disastrous storm in 1881 in which a tidal wave swamped most of the quarries, both on Easdale Island and at

Flooded quarry

Ellenabeich, Mr McColl resigned. His replacement was Mr Wilson, a gentleman of much greater energy and enterprise, who set about the task of putting the Easdale quarries into as full production as was possible following the storm damage. The large Ellenabeich quarry, already nearly worked out before the flooding, was abandoned and much of the machinery transferred to the island of Easdale. Quarries at Balvicar and on Luing were largely unaffected by the storm and now began to provide the bulk of the slate exported. In the last decade of the century the MacLean brothers, Joseph and Alan, leased the Luing and Balvicar quarries and, despite a series of industrial disputes, production continued more or less successfully until the outbreak of the Great War in 1914.

In collaboration with the local doctor, Dr Patrick Gillies, Mr Wilson cleaned up Easdale Island and the villages of Balvicar and Ellenabeich, improving both sanitation and housing. He and the doctor were both active members of the Volunteers, a force of civilians which had been set up in the 1860s to defend Britain from threat of invasion by the French. Through this organisation the two men were able to enlist the support of the quarry workforce to carry out improvements which required voluntary work, such as digging drains, erecting a wooden hospital building and so forth.

Despite Major Wilson's important contribution to the Easdale Slate Quarrying Company, the Easdale quarries never again approached the levels of production of former years and finally succumbed to competition from both Ballachulish and the Welsh slate quarries, and also from cheap imports from abroad. Additional reasons for the failure of the quarries were more complex. The South African (Boer) War took a number of the younger men from the district, while the discovery of gold in Africa, America and Australia lured men skilled in mining work to seek their fortunes overseas. Changes in architectural design meant that clay tiles increasingly replaced slate for roofing, and the lack of a rail link between Oban and Easdale prevented the cheap transport of slates overland.

The last slates to be taken from the Easdale quarries on a commercial scale were shipped in 1911. Other quarries in the district survived for longer periods. The Balvicar quarry was revived as recently as the late 1940s and continued operating until the early '60s.

There is little information available about the slate quarrying on Belnahua, lying to the SW of Easdale and NW of Luing. It was, and still is, a privately owned island whose one claim to fame was the export of many thousands of good quality roofing slates during the final decade of the 19th century. Two large quarries occupy the centre of the island and on the rim a small village, now entirely ruined, was built to house the workers and their families. There was no piped water supply and insufficient land to grow food crops. Islanders had to be sustained in all things by boat from Cullipool on Luing. The declaration of war in August 1914 left the island without any men of working age. The houses were abandoned and the population dispersed. Nothing but the gable ends of a few ruined buildings remain to tell us of the harsh lives experienced by this tiny community. Today the island offers the visitor arriving by boat a view of water-filled quarries, a ghost village and a unique habitat for wildlife.

As the quarries began to close, the younger people left to seek work elsewhere. Some went to quarries further south; many more emigrated to British colonies overseas where connections had already been made through the slate trade. It is the descendants of these emigrants who form a large proportion of today's overseas visitors.

CHAPTER 3

Winning the Slate

THE NATURAL CLEAVAGE EXHIBITED by slate rock ensures that when it is split using appropriate tools, large flat sheets of rock can be obtained. So tough is the rock that these sheets may be split to between 12mm and 6mm without breaking up. A skilful cutter can cut across the cleavage to produce slates of the required sizes for roofing purposes.

Traditionally these sizes are named as follows:

Princess	600x350mm
*Duchess	600x300mm
*Countess	500x250mm
Ladies	400x200mm
Headers	350x300mm
Doubles	300x150mm
*Sizeable	250x125mm
*Undersize	125x63mm

* sizes recorded in the Easdale journals.

While awaiting loading, cut slates were stacked, according to size, between a series of vertically placed slate slabs. Looking like so many grave stones, a group of these can still be seen standing on the north side of Easdale harbour.

The earliest quarrying took place on the shore, where the slate had been exposed by the natural activity of the waves. As the shoreline was denuded to below sea level, it became increasingly difficult to keep out the water even at low tide. By building a system of walls and sluices, the quarriers were able to control the flow of water and worked in relatively dry, safe conditions for a few hours each day, tides and daylight permitting. As the quarries fell further below sea level, walls were built to keep out the sea at all times.

One of these, 4 metres in height, stands on the seaward side of one of the largest quarries on the west side of Easdale Island. Similar structures were built at Ellenabeich. The action of the sea is gradually removing the one remaining wall, but so well was it constructed that a small section has survived, although untended, since the quarries closed nearly a century ago. Further evidence of masonry to maintain the rim of the quarries can be seen on the NE side of the Windmill Quarry to the N of Easdale Island. Reinforcement using concrete was introduced late in the 19th century and can be seen in one quarry. This dates the quarry to about 1890 when MacAlpine was introducing concrete for civil engineering works throughout Scotland.

The largest exposures on Luing are above sea level and could not easily be worked by the water-soaked wedge method employed at Easdale and Ellenabeich. The fine quality slate at Cullipool could be mined successfully only after the introduction of gunpowder.

Following the establishment of the Marble and Slate Company of Netherlorn in 1745, various forms of mechanisation were introduced both to remove water from the quarries and to transport the rock. The waste rock which constituted as much as sixty percent of the material quarried, created its own problems of disposal. At first the spoil was spread over the surface of unquarried ground. Later, as quarries became abandoned because the sea could no longer be excluded, the waste was shovelled into the disused pits. Occasionally a good use was found for the waste in producing causeways and embankments for access purposes and for infilling pitted ground to make space for building accommodation for the workers and their families. This infilling process was responsible for joining Eilean na Beich (Isle of Birches) to the Isle of Seil and providing a suitable foundation for the houses in that village.

The most unsatisfactory solution to the problem of disposing of slate waste was to tip the spoil into the sea as happened on the west side of Easdale Island. Embankments were built running outwards to the farthest points west, with railway track to carry the trolleys filled with waste. The action of the tides has moved this material around the island to build up the mole of loose slate which forms a low beach of slate shingle facing the shoreline of Seil across Easdale Sound. This loose rock, moving southwards along the Sound at every spring tide and during stormy weather, regularly blocks the entrance to Easdale harbour, necessitating dredging it at least once a year.

In the earliest days the women and children, with creels upon their backs, carried the made slates to the harbour for stacking. When John Whyte was appointed grieve in 1840, he built a system of railway lines between the quarries and the harbour, and also across the floor of each of the quarries, which made haulage simpler. The trolleys were dragged at first by men and later by horses. According to eyewitness accounts, small locomotives were used on these same tracks from 1860 onwards. On Easdale Island both horses and locomotives were housed in the coalree, one of only two industrial buildings still in use on the island. Remains of the railway track, removed in recent times from other parts of the island for sale as scrap, can be seen embedded in the coalree floor. For some tasks, no suitable alternative was ever found for the horse, teams of Clydesdales being employed until the Easdale quarries closed down in 1911.

From the earliest records, we know that slate rock was removed from the foreshore by inserting hardwood wedges in natural cracks in the slate at low tide. As the tide rose, the wedges swelled and the cracks widened. Skilful placement of the wedges meant that the rock would split into manageable blocks after a number of tides. Once broken out, the block was hauled above high water mark for splitting and napping, or trimming, into roofing slates. When sea-water could no longer be used to break out the slate, gunpowder was introduced. The levels of blasting were very critical because too much force would shatter the rock and render it useless for cutting.

Keeping gunpowder dry must have been a particular problem. There is evidence that both powder and fuses were kept in some cottages. A bag of live fuses, which had remained undisturbed for 70 years, was discovered in the loft of one of the cottages in 1980.

Quarrier at work drilling holes
for blasting

An army bomb disposal officer was brought in to remove them and explode them in safety.

From the days of the Marble and Slate Company of Nletherlorn, various methods of pumping the quarries had been tried. One early experiment in this respect was the Newcomen Atmospheric Engine by means of which water could be lifted from a low to a higher level. The introduction of this piece of machinery was viewed by the simple islanders with awe and amazement. Some parties who witnessed the performance stated, however, that its operation was quite unsatisfactory, which was hardly surprising considering the fact that the boiler was a square box made of 1 inch thick cast iron and its piston was packed with leather. The mighty beam operated by the Newcomen engine required a special, tall structure to house

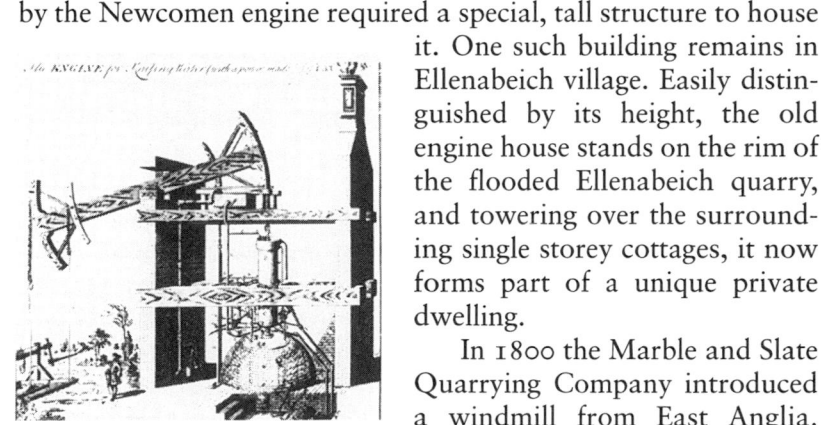

Pumping engine as used from
1745 onwards

it. One such building remains in Ellenabeich village. Easily distinguished by its height, the old engine house stands on the rim of the flooded Ellenabeich quarry, and towering over the surrounding single storey cottages, it now forms part of a unique private dwelling.

In 1800 the Marble and Slate Quarrying Company introduced a windmill from East Anglia. This was set up in the most northerly of the quarries on

Easdale Island, which to this day is known as the Windmill Quarry. From time to time steam driven pumping gear was acquired locally from wrecked vessels, naval equipment being of infinitely better quality than anything the Company could afford in the normal course of events. The remains of Currie's Engine House, built following the great storm of 1881, can still be seen on the west side of the Easdale hill together with the boiler house which provided steam to work the equipment. Close by is a ruined forge.

Currie's Engine House, Easdale, c.1889

When the large quarry at Ellenabeich was flooded, much valuable equipment was lost, but Mr Wilson, the new manager, retrieved the large crane and several smaller winches and installed them on Easdale Island. Platforms built to hold this equipment can be found near all the quarries, and the occasional rusty piece of iron sticking up out of the ground indicates the extent of the piped steam system employed.

Men worked in teams of five or six; two quarriers, two splitters and trimmers (nappers), and two labourers whose job it was to supply the nappers with rock and remove the finished slates and the spoil.

Those dressing the slate worked as close to the rock face as was practicable. They created for themselves rectangular pits in the ground, neatly reinforced with dry stone walling. Corner posts supported a canvas or corrugated iron roof which kept out the wind and rain while they worked. All over the district such pits can still be seen in the proximity of the quarries. In this crude shelter the men, often seated in the water which collected around them as they worked, split and shaped the slates throughout the hours of daylight. It is little wonder that the most prevalent diseases amongst the quarrymen were rheumatism and arthritis.

The men were paid by the thousand slates sold, the different trades attracting different wages, with quarrymen being considered the most highly skilled. In the early days, the gangs were paid twice yearly and were obliged to run up a bill with the Company store in the meantime. A tally was kept of the number of slates made by the gang and of amounts owing at the store. There were literally recorded by writing on a slate. Hence the term *'put it on the slate.'*

Casual workers were paid a daily rate and received their money whether or not the slate was sold. Although they received less money than the regular workers, they were seen to have an advantage and this discrepancy in methods of payment was the subject of disputes recorded in the Company papers.

From the early days of the Marble and Slate Company of Netherlorn, it had been the accepted tradition that the men were paid only after the slates had been sold and shipped. Towards the end of the 18th century, after the quarries had been working steadily for 50 years, despite a good trade in exporting to the colonies, a considerable stockpile of slate had been amassed for which the men had received no payment. In the Company Minutes of 28 August 1799 the following entry appears under Item 18:

> Agreed to give a present of 40,000 slates to the Infirmary of Glasgow from the Company and the quarriers allowed their share of the slate.

One wonders if the men had any say in this matter. It was the directors of the Company who received the accolades for this generous gesture!

Towards the end of the 19th century when the various quarries had been leased to consortia of businessmen, an agreement was in force by which the men were to be paid eight times a year. Trouble broke out when the men, having received only their fifth payment in one year in the month of November, threatened industrial action.

At Cullipool, on Luing, where the men refused to load slates aboard ship before they received their pay, the Company moved in blackleg labour to do the work. With threats of violence, the quarrymen stood their ground while the managers resorted to the local 'riot police' to keep control. Fortunately the blacklegs, once appraised of the quarrymen's case, sympathised with it and quietly dispersed.

Oban Times, 12 August 1893:

Cullipool: The strike in connection with the slate quarries here has been, writes our correspondent, maintained for the last three weeks with the utmost vigour and quite successfully as far as the men are concerned. It is the custom in the quarries here that all the slates made by each squad are shipped before the contract time is up. However, this part of the work has been stoutly refused by the men, although a vessel has been waiting for a cargo for the last fortnight. It may be noted that the works at Toberonochy also is leased by Mssrs MacLean and last week Mssrs J & A MacLean made a strong appeal to the men there to come and ship the slate at Cullipool. Not withstanding every inducement offered, the crews promptly refused to have anything to do with the Cullipool men's affairs. At last however, a few individuals about Toberonochy were prevailed upon to go to Cullipool to load the vessel lying there. They were assured also that in the event of a hostile demonstration on the part of the strikers, police protection would be forthcoming. Accordingly Superintendent MacIntyre, Oban, and a number of policemen made their appearance in Cullipool on Monday. Seven (Toberonochy) men out of about sixty put in an appearance.
The whole of the Cullipool men turned out and it was feared for some time that there might be a disturbance between the strikers and those from Toberonochy. Any demonstration was fortunately avoided by the good sense shown by the Cullipool men, who with a good deal of banter prevailed on the Toberonochy men to retire, which they did without handling any slate...

Each gang of six men was allocated a section of the quarry in which to work. During the 1880s, at which time the Easdale Slate Quarrying Company was sub-let by the Breadalbane Estates to a consortium of Glasgow businessmen, lack of investment and poor overseeing by the manager, Mr McColl, led to the use of too many gangs operating at each new face. The groups of men got in each other's way as they blasted and levered the rock from the quarry walls. Serious accidents were common, at least one proving fatal.

Oban Times, 31 December 1887:

The following petition drawn up by the quarriers of Easdale, detailing their grievances and seeking for a remedy, was forwarded some weeks ago to the Marquis of Breadalbane.

To the Most Noble, the Marquis of Breadalbane, humbly showeth

1. That we beg leave to call your Lordship's attention to a serious accident which occurred at the Balvicar Slate Quarries, the result being that one man was killed, one seriously injured, while others had a narrow escape.

2. That when some of these men made objections to go to work at this place because of overcrowding, they were told by the Company's manager that unless they took the work offered there was no other for them.

3. That the Company has been warned several times that this system of overcrowding is dangerous to life and limb.

4. That after having thus overcrowded us, there are always a number of unemployed, about twenty in all, and some of these have been idle for three months.

5. That under the present circumstances we find we are unable to earn a livelihood.

6. That we would beg leave to ask your Lordship to be good enough to make provision whereby those going idle shall get employment. Or is it your Lordship's desire that such shall be starved out of the place?

7. That as far as we can see the remedy must be something apart altogether from that of the Easdale Slate Company.

Trusting your Lordship will kindly take this, our petition, into your favourable consideration,

We are etc. ...

Since the Easdale quarries officially closed in 1911 attempts have been made on a very small scale to continue to win slate from a number of quarries in the district. The material obtained has been used in the main for monumental and craft purposes only. At Balvicar, Toberonochy and Cullipool, quarrying continued until the outbreak of the Great War in 1914. Slate quarrying not being a trade considered essential to the war effort, quarrymen throughout the district were recruited for the Armed Services, leaving only old men and boys to work the quarries. Several attempts were made to re-open the quarries at Balvicar and on Luing during the 20th century and other Scottish slate quarries such as those at Ballachulish, Aberfoyle and Luss, which had better communications by rail, continued for a while longer, but the market for slate had diminished with the import of cheap continental slate, machine-cut Welsh slate and, in particular, Dutch clay tiles which could be produced in a variety of colours. It was economic considerations as well as mechanisation which, combined with the whim of the architectural schools up and down the country, finally destroyed one of Scotland's greatest industries and largely depopulated Argyll's largest industrial centre. Ellenabeich, Easdale, Balvicar and the Luing villages are conservation villages in which many of the houses are listed buildings. Roof repairs and extensions must now be carried out in slate or a suitable substitute (made from reconstituted slate dust). In recent times Easdale slates have been recovered from dismantled buildings in Glasgow and elsewhere in order to carry out repairs and renovations. Despite having been exposed to the polluting atmosphere of the city for more than 100 years, these recycled Easdale slates have been found to be in good condition and are expected to continue to give unlimited service.

CHAPTER 4

Housing

WHEN THE MARBLE AND Slate Company of Netherlorn was formed in 1745, it was agreed that the men brought in to work the quarries would require housing of a good standard. The earliest cottages were built of the local stone which included the slate rock and the hard Dolerite, or whinstone. The houses were of one or two rooms and almost certainly thatched, using either reed or heather. Any windows were shuttered rather than glazed and the cooking fire would have been vented through a hole in the centre of the roof.

Towards the end of the 18th century, the Company agreed to provide slate for roofing the cottages and coal was introduced to replace the peat fires. In changing the roof design, a stone or brick built chimney was included to accommodate a cooking range. The slates used for roofing were those which were the least saleable, namely of the sizeable and undersized sizes. It is wrong, however, to assume from this, as have certain historians reporting on the industry, that all Easdale roofing slates were small. The larger sizes were exported!

In the 1850s the Marquis of Breadalbane, noting complaints from the quarrymen about the inadequacy of housing, engaged an architect to design an additional group of cottages in Ellenabeich. Copies of the plans for these dwellings can be studied in the Easdale Island Folk Museum and confirm the original layout of the cottages. Unfortunately the new cottages were never built, although many of the existing buildings seem to have been upgraded to a similar standard. The addition of a porch, however, as shown in the drawings, was not included. Today's residents very much regret this omission. Planning rules demand that the front elevation of the cottages shall not be altered and porches are generally not allowed.

One of the few cottages left in its 19th C. original condition

For their period, these buildings were considered superior housing for working men. Each consisted of two rooms with a central lobby and behind it a wall bed, usually accessed from the kitchen. The roof space, although hardly high enough for a man to stand upright at the centre, was used as a sleeping place for children. A skylight made of isinglass or other translucent material lit the attic, while small panes of glass were introduced in the ordinary windows to provide natural lighting. Some houses had their own outside privies with slate slabs for roofing.

Houses were let to quarry workers at a rent which over the years, when records are available, reflected the current prosperity of the community. In 1897 a quarterly rent of 12/4d [62p] was charged, but by 1911 this had reduced to 5/- [25p] per annum.

When the quarrying company was finally dissolved, the Breadalbane Estates offered the houses to their tenants for sale at the cost of a year's rent. Some of these houses have been handed down through the generations and are still in the hands of direct descendants of the quarry workers. When the Breadalbane Estates were finally disbanded in the 1930s, the Slate Villages were almost deserted, only a sprinkling of permanent residents remaining. In the summer months their numbers were swelled by former quarrying families who had moved away to find work but returned for holidays, usually for the Glasgow Fair (Glasgow Trade Holidays). Even today during the last two weeks in July every house on each of the Slate Islands seems to be bursting at the seams.

When the Breadalbane Estates were sold up, there was a much wider distribution of property in the district, although the agricultural land and coarse grazing tended to be in the hands of just a few wealthy land owners.

A good example of what became of the dwelling houses is illustrated by the fate of buildings on Easdale Island. Donald Dewer purchased Easdale Island in the late 1950s. He reconstructed some of the cottages to let as holiday homes, and others had their roofs removed to avoid paying rates. When Donald Dewer accidentally drowned in the harbour, his successor, Peter Fennel, made serious attempts to restore the cottages, rebuilding many with his own hands and with the help of local craftsmen. Over the years these reconstructed houses have changed ownership, often

Traditional quarry workers' cottages, Easdale Island

several times, and the improvements have continued. Today the majority of cottages have been renovated to the highest standards, being centrally heated, double glazed and with all modern conveniences. None of the houses remain in the possession of the present owner of Easdale Island, Clive Feigenbaum. Most are owned, together with their garden ground, by their occupiers.

Before the Slate Island villages became designated Conservation Areas in the late 1970s, little attention was paid by the Planning Department of Argyll Council to the materials being used to reconstruct the houses. Hence many buildings in the district have been roofed using cheap composition tiles; windows are of various sizes and forms; and several houses have an abnormal roof pitch. Now that Conservation Areas have been designated, all new work in these is carefully vetted. Planners insist that as well as slate, or a good slate substitute, for roofing, sliding sash, timber-framed windows, and a traditional façade must be used. Where owners have decided to convert their houses to central heating, foregoing the use of open fires, they are nevertheless required to provide a false chimney to conform with the standard outward appearance of the buildings. While it is hoped that most of the 20th century anomalies in building construction will eventually be removed, it is important to realise that the villages do not look only to the past. While wishing to preserve the appearance of housing for the sake of informing and educating future generations, the islanders insist upon the right to improve their homes to the highest modern standards, albeit in a sensitive manner. Today, only a sprinkling of houses are without mains water and septic tank drainage. Most have their kitchens equipped with every modern device for cooking and cleaning, and while bathrooms are usually small, a number of houses can boast a jacuzzi and in some there is even a sauna.

CHAPTER 5

Public Health

THE GENERAL HEALTH OF the islanders appears to have been exceptionally good for most of the period for which records exist. A survey conducted in 1791 describes a population healthy, in good spirits and above average in intelligence. Smallpox had been eradicated by a system of inoculation introduced many years before Edward Jenner claimed responsibility for the introduction of vaccination against the disease in 1796.

The local doctor, who was engaged by the Slate Quarrying Company, was principally responsible for the health of the workmen, attending to their injuries whether in the quarries or at sea. In the 19th century we find that the men paid a small sum annually for which they obtained medical care for themselves and their families. Confinements were extra, a charge of 10/6 [53p] being levied. This meant that many births were supervised only by the village midwife, an untrained female who also provided traditional remedies for all ailments.

The most prevalent diseases were arthritis and rheumatism brought on by working usually up to the ankles in water and often in the rain and chilling winds. When in the 1880s the slate industry began to fail, poverty, poor sanitation and overcrowding resulted in many cases of tuberculosis. At this time cities in Scotland were visited by another virulent disease, cholera. The only instance of the disease amongst the Slate Islands occurred when a visitor from Glasgow, here to recuperate, suffered a relapse.

Working in water without waterproof footwear

Infant mortality rates were high throughout the 19th century. A large number of children never reached their first birthday. Often the same name was applied to more than one child in a family, to ensure continuity.

The most valuable records of public health in the district are the annual reports of Dr Patrick H Gillies compiled from 1890 until 1910 during which time he was the Medical Officer for the Easdale Slate Quarrying Company. These records provide a fascinating account of life in the Parish of Kilbrandon and Kilchattan at that time.

Patrick's concern about the poor sanitary condition of the quarrying villages is illustrated by the following extract from his annual report to the Medical Officer for Heath, Argyll, January 1896:

> During the months of September and October we had a visit of what is now our annual visitor, Typhoid fever.
>
> The cases, three in number, all occurred in Ellenabeich but whereas in former years the cases were all confined to children, this year it attacked three grown up people of strong and healthy situation and was of a very severe type. Fortunately no death occurred but this is due to the most diligent situation and careful nursing on the part of the attendants. Fairly good isolation and thorough disinfection of the excreta and formities were, I believe instrumental in preventing the spread of the disease. ...
>
> ... I mention a series of facts which I think will lead one to discover the cause of the trouble and its persistence here.
>
> While the old Ellenabeich quarry was being worked, the water pumped from the quarry was conveyed from the pump to the sea by an open gutter a foot or more in depth, which passes through the main street of the village into the mouth of the dock. There was sufficient water to flush the drain and any sewage thrown into it was immediately carried to sea. In 1881 the quarry was flooded and work ceased. The gutter still remained an open gutter but although sewage was still thrown in without there being any flushing of the pump water, the sewage did no harm and it seemed that the surface

drainage, aided by occasional bucketsful from the inhabitants, managed to keep the drain clean. No bad effects resulted.

After some years the Parochial Board, then the Local Authority, determined to do away with this gutter and have a deep enclosed drain constructed, thereby to improve the health of the village.

A local contractor was employed and a drain measuring about 500ft. in length was constructed beginning at the N end of the Main Street opposite the Post Office door, running for 300ft. the length of the street ... down Main Street, then turning at right angles and passing between two blocks of houses to its outlet in the old quarry, where it never discharged its contents.

Its total course is 500ft. and as far as I can make out by taking levels, roughly the fall in that length is 2ft 6ins or of one half percent.

There is no means of flushing the drain. Small effects pass to each door along the street and slops and mire are its only contents. The drain is roughly built of slabs of slate embedded in the slate spoil on which the houses of this part of the village are built.

The drain was constructed in 1888 and the next year, 1889, the first case of Typhoid appeared. In 1890 there was a second. In 1892 three cases broke out, in 1894 there was one case and in 1895, three. In all, nine cases of Typhoid fever in six infected houses. All these houses lie on the NE side of Main Street. Not one house on the south side has, as far as I know, been affected. It is peculiar that out of a row of houses containing twelve houses, five these should have harboured the infection.

The South row of houses is built on slate rock. The North row is built on slate spoil. The drain is about mid way between. Also, in the slate spoil the ground slopes from the S to the N.

During the hot periods of this year such as we experienced in September 1895, when the last cases occurred, the prevailing wind is SSW. Should any infection arise from the drain, the moist foggy atmosphere should be a capital carrier. The prevailing wind blows fog and germs through the doors and windows, which the inhabitants have left wide open in the heat of the day. It may be that the infection is spread in the soil water which trickles through, and from the rain draining through the spoil beneath the houses.

There has been no Typhoid in Front Row which was built on slate spoil (but had no drain)

Ellenabeich village street today

Patrick demonstrates the current thinking about the spread of infectious disease. Weight was still given to the idea that noxious air might bring germs into a house. He does however come to the more probable explanation for the disease affecting only one side of the street: the flow of water carrying infected material from the roughly constructed drain into the slate spoil below the houses. In Ellenabeich the water was collected in rain butts and from several burns flowing through the village and it is highly likely that these sources were contaminated by the infected ground water. A rather inadequate reservoir built on the hill above Ellenabeich had been constructed to serve the quarry machinery, and water was conducted to Easdale Island by pipe under the ocean. Stand pipes from this reservoir were used by the Easdale islanders. Since there were no reported cases of typhoid on Easdale Island, one must assume that the reservoir water was not contaminated.

For many years Patrick Gillies pursued the idea of a small isolation hospital where his contagious patients could be kept apart from other members of the family. The cottages often housed two parents, several children and maybe a grandparent as well, all living in two rooms and perhaps using the loft space for sleeping. It was not uncommon for there to be six or seven people living in one cottage. In response to Patrick's regular requests, a Docker Hut, a wooden prefabricated building, was eventually supplied.

Dr Patrick Gillies

Since it had only one ward and no accommodation for a nurse, it was inadequate to say the least. The construction of this building was completed a week or two after an epidemic of typhoid had swept through Ellenabeich village. By the time the hospital was ready for occupation, all the patients had recovered. The following year, just before a second epidemic broke out, the building was swept away in a gale and ended up strewn along the beaches as far away as Cuan village. Eventually the Authorities acceded to Patrick's initial demand that he be allowed to make use of the disused church at Cuan. After much correspondence and considerable argument, he was able to take possession of the building, which had accommodation for both men and women, and a nurse was appointed. For a number of years the isolation hospital proved a great asset to the villages and was disbanded only when the population became so denuded that the facility was no longer viable.

Dr Gillies took an active part in all aspects of Parish life. He was fluent in the Gaelic tongue and compiled a history of the district, *Netherlorn And Its Neighbourhood*, much of his information taken from ancient Gaelic writings. For his literary achievements he was made a member of the Royal Society of Arts. Until his death in 1931, Patrick supported the movement to have Gaelic spoken in the churches and restored to the school curriculum. He was Honorary Surgeon to the 1st (Easdale) Artillery Volunteer Company and served for a short time in the army in South Africa during the Boer War.

In his role as Medical Officer for the Easdale quarries, Gillies negotiated improved terms for the prepayment scheme for medical treatment, a forerunner of the Liberal Party's Panel system which was introduced at a much later date. He was also an active member of the Parochial Council, administering subsidies to the poor of the district and negotiating transfers to the workhouse.

Patrick Gillies practised preventative medicine before the discipline had acquired a name. Believing that the health of the community should begin with the health of the children, he made periodic inspections at all the schools in the parish and drew up regulations for the isolation of infectious children. His work in the schools, including a plethora of correspondence with officers of the Argyll Council, brought him to the notice of others concerned with the preventative aspects of child health. In 1912 he was appointed Medical Officer for Schools in Scotland. His final post was that of Medical Officer of Health for Argyll.

Patrick Gillies died at Connel in 1931, aged 62 years.

The Gillies family provided medical care for the district for several generations, most of the male members becoming doctors. Patrick's father, Hugh Gillies, was the Easdale doctor in the 1870s. His obelisk is to be found in the old cemetery at Balvicar, standing alongside the graves of his sons, Hunter, John and Patrick. A fourth son, Hugh, was a noted Gaelic scholar who distinguished himself in his medical studies at both Edinburgh University and Glasgow Infirmary and founded a second Gillies dynasty of doctors.

Dunmore House, Easdale – home of the Gillies doctors

Alexander Gillies, Patrick's son, practised medicine in Macclesfield for very many years. He excelled in sport playing full-back for Scotland in the rugby football teams of the late 1920s and early '30s, and was a noted figure in golfing circles. Alexander's daughter, Fiona, a frequent visitor to the island, became a State Registered Nurse, and her brother Patrick was medical officer for a gold mining company in South Africa until his retirement a few years ago. His son, Hunter, qualified as a doctor in 1997.

Other branches of the family have also produced a succession of medical men, one of whom, Malcolm Gillies, founded the town of Bowen in Queensland, Australia.

Today the GP for the Easdale area, George Hannah, lives at Finlaggan on the Easdale road north of Balvicar. He covers much the same ground as his Victorian predecessors serving the islands of Seil, Luing and Easdale with occasional calls to Scarba, Fladda and other such isolated spots. Although his journeys around the parish are by four-wheel drive vehicle rather than on horseback, he is as likely to be called out to make a sea crossing in the darkest hours on a winter's night as were his predecessors. With the facility of a fine new hospital in Oban, an excellent ambulance service and recourse to a helicopter when necessary, patients can be transferred rapidly to receive treatment at the hands of specialist consultants, but nevertheless, the people of this isolated region depend for their primary care and first aid upon their GP. Following in the footsteps of Patrick Gillies, Dr Hannah believes in prevention in preference to cure and woe betide any of his patients who miss regular check-ups or neglect to avail themselves of any national screening programs. Visitors who find themselves in need of medical assistance are often amazed at the speed with which help arrives in the form of a tall, bearded figure in polo-necked sweater and, as like as not, clad in oilskins against the weather or in preparation for sailing. When a tourist injured her leg while climbing the hill on Easdale Island recently, it was found necessary to lift her off by helicopter. Sadly, George did not get his greatly anticipated flight to Oban with her because there was insufficient room on board!

The population of the parish of Kilbrandon and Kilchattan increases year by year and medical services have become stretched to their limit. In 1999 a new surgery and treatment centre was opened close to Finlaggan House. Here Dr Hannah and his partner, together with a small team of nurses and paramedics, carry out their primary care duties, the centre providing improved facilities for the various clinics which have been initiated over the years.

CHAPTER 6

Religion in Netherlorn

The Parishes of Kilbrandon and Kilchattan

FOR AN ACCOUNT OF the earliest records of Christianity in Netherlorn we are indebted to Patrick H Gillies MB., FSA Scot., who was the Medical Officer to the Easdale Slate Quarrying Company for more than twenty years between 1890 and 1912. Patrick, a native Gaelic speaker, was born at Dunmore House on the Isle of Seil and attended the village school at Ellenabeich until he was sent to George Watson's School in Edinburgh at the age of eleven. Thence he went on to Edinburgh University to study Medicine.

In compiling his history of the area, *Netherlorn and its Neighbourhood*, Dr Gillies was able to refer to ancient works in their original Gaelic and his sources are quoted as Adamnan, Columba's biographer whose work was translated by Bishop Reves, as well as Dean Munro (1549), Martin Martin (1695), Pennant (1772) and McCulloch (1819), all of whom recorded journeys around the Western Isles. Other historians quoted by Gillies include Skene, Gregory, Dr Dugald Mitchell, Cosmo Innes and Dr Christison.

There is evidence to show that Christianity arrived in Netherlorn some considerable time before St Columba was exiled from Ireland in 563 and began his mission to convert the Picts to Christianity.

St Brendan was trained in the same seminary, founded by St Finnian in Clonard in Ireland, from which Columba was to emerge many years later. In the second quarter of the 6th century he travelled along the western coast of Scotland establishing chapels and Christian settlements as he went. The first of these, completed in 542, was a monastery at Eileach a' Naoimh (Rock of Saints), the most westerly of the Garvelloch Isles. A few years later he founded the Church of Kilbrandon in Lorn.

The remains of the ancient chapel attributed to St Brendan in Kilbrandon churchyard

The original chapel of St Brendan is thought to have been at Suidhe Bhreanain (Brendan's resting place), in the North of the parish to the west of Loch Seil. The site was probably chosen deliberately to coincide with a much earlier religious settlement, for nearby are the remains of a megalithic stone circle thought to have been constructed by the Druids.

Brendan was already an old man by the time Columba, exiled from Ireland for his political leanings, landed at Knapdale and built a chapel in Kintyre at the head of Loch Killisport. Two years later Columba sailed to Aileach a Naoimh on route to the North where he established his main base on Iona. Columba was thought to have had a special affinity with Eileach a' Naoimh which he used as a retreat on several occasions. Thought to have been the Hinbar mentioned by Columba's biographer as his favourite retreat, the monastery was for many years run by his uncle, Ernan, and is the burial place of his mother, Aethne. Now under the protection of Historic Scotland, the substantial ruins of extraordinary beehive-shaped buildings have been quite well preserved over the centuries.

From Brendan's first landing on Seil until the Reformation in Scotland, all Christian worship was based on Rome. A church whose establishment is attributed to Brendan himself was built in the centre of Seil Island, close to Kilbrandon House.

In Seil's ancient kirkyard, a few yards to the south of the Balvicar crossroads, can be seen a convex structure in masonry thought to be the roof of the crypt of a medieval chapel. Several ancient gravestones exist nearby bearing the traditional Celtic symbols of interlaced one, two, or three strand plaits, loops large and small, and floral and leaf designs. Centrally, some symbol denotes the occupation of the deceased: ... a claymore, a crozier and in one case a pair of scissors or shears.

During the centuries when the Roman Catholic Church held sway in Netherlorn, an important centre for its activities was the township of Kilbride which still exists today as Kilbride Farm and the complex of holiday cottages and chalets called Kilbride Croft, both of which stand on the brow of the hill on the Easdale Road, west of the Balvicar Crossroads. Kilbride remained in the feu of the Roman Catholic Church from the time of St Brendan until, as a result of the Reformation in Scotland, all lands belonging to the Church were redistributed. The township was placed in the care of Patrick MacLachlan who, having embraced the principles of the Reformation, was considered a worthy recipient of the King's favour.

The MacLachlan family had been closely associated with the Medieval Roman Church for generations. Farquar MacLachlan was the penultimate pre-Reformation Bishop of the Isles, while many other members of the family acted as vicars in the parish. With the church lands at Kilbride, Patrick MacLachlan inherited a substantial part of the library removed from the monastery on Iona at its dissolution in the 1530s. The Kilbride Manuscripts are a voluminous collection of ancient Gaelic writings very much valued by ecclesiastical historians. In the early 19th century the manuscripts were placed in the Advocates' Library in Edinburgh by Major MacLachlan of the 55th Foot, the then proprietor of the Kilbride Township.

Balvicar (Baile bhiocair, the vicar's township) was also church property until the Reformation, when it was gifted to the Campbells of Calder, a branch of Clan Campbell united to the Thanes of Cawdor by the marriage of Muriel to one of the sons of the Earl of Argyll.

The Reformation saw the establishment of the Church of Scotland and the building of three new churches in the parish. At the north end of the parish, North Church was built, overlooking Loch Feochan. On the southern tip of the Isle of Seil a second church was built at Cuan. Both of these buildings still exist and are in use as private houses. The little church at Cuan, which is still recognisable because of its bell tower, stood empty for some time after the present Kilbrandon Church was consecrated in 1866, until in the 1890s Patrick Gillies was successful in persuading the Local Authority to convert it into an isolation hospital.

The third church or chapel was at Kilchattan, towards the southern end of the island of Luing. The chapel ruins can still be seen today, near the site of the present Kilchattan Church.

Alexander Beith DD, one-time Minister of the parish of Kilbrandon and Kilchattan, wrote in 1845 in his book *A Highland Tour*:

> We had passed in our romantic sail from Crinan, the Slate Isles where, for about four years, I had been the Minister. In the distance, to the east, as we sped along towards the north, the old parish church at Cuan was visible. I pointed it out to my friends.
>
> The rapidity of the tide as it rushes through this strait, narrowed by the projecting shores of the island of Seil on the one hand and of Luing on the other, always great, is sometimes quite terrific.
>
> It was often a cheering sight to witness on a Sabbath morning, the vast fleet of slate-makers' boats from the islands of Easdale and Ellenabeich, crowded with men, women and children, coming to attend

church, sweep through this pass, floating on the raging tide, scarcely needing the use of oars but to guide their course; no return being possible until the ebbing waters had come back exhausted, and until, changing their course, they had come back in full flood to carry home again, with an equally small expense of toil, the crowds which in the interval had worshipped in the Temple of God. Alternately, the parishioners on the eastern portion of my charge enjoyed this advantage, when those from the other side then required to travel by road.

The Church of Scotland was now the only church in the parish of Kilbrandon and Kilchattan. It played a major role in all aspects of community life providing both education for the young and support for the old and needy. The living was in the gift of the major landowner, The Earl of Breadalbane, and successive Earls appear to have fulfilled their philanthropic role satisfactorily. Those who worked in the Earl's slate quarries being particularly well served.

Despite the large concentration of people on Easdale Island (450 in 1860), even at the height of the Company's prosperity there was never a permanent place of worship on that island. Evangelistic preachers did visit it from time to time and there are accounts of a tent having to be erected to keep the preacher safe from the elements. Today, during the summer season when the island is well populated, it is not uncommon for the Minister to hold an occasional Sunday meeting in the Puffer Tea Room.

In the years following the death of Henry VIII, there was a concerted move to return to Roman Catholicism, but Easdale was far from the seat of Government whether in Edinburgh or London, and changes came about slowly. As the pendulum swung back and forth between Catholicism and Protestantism, groups formed and reformed, church buildings came and went and with them a series of houses described as The Manse. Several of the older houses in the district bear that title, for example at Ellenabeich, Sea View, Ballachuan and Cuan. The present Manse stands opposite the entrance to the ancient cemetery of Kilbrandon and was built in 1992.

By 1690 we find the Church of Scotland occupying the North and South Churches already described. The Covenanters, a group of Presbyterians who broke away from the Church of Scotland soon after the Reformation and were as opposed to the role of the monarch as the Head of the Church as they were to Papacy in all its forms, has an establishment at Ballachuan on the Cuan Road, while the Scottish Episcopal Church is still firmly entrenched at Kilbride.

The Covenanters survived in the district until the 1870s, by which time their main stronghold was on Luing. Their rules were too harsh for many liberal minded Easdale men, and membership, never large, soon began to fall away when, late in the 19th century, efforts were made to reconcile the various factions which had divided off from the Church of Scotland.

There was no Episcopalian place of worship on Luing when, late in the 19th century, a group of quarriers and their families arrived from Ballachulish to work in the quarries at Cullipool. The men, strictly adhering to their Episcopalian ideals, built their own small church on a hill overlooking the village. Today it too is a private residence. The Episcopalian Church survived at Kilbride on Seil until 1930, at which time the congregation was so small that separate church premises were no longer warranted. With better transport, including a local bus, it was possible for Episcopalians to travel to Oban to worship.

The Disruption of 1843 had left the Church of Scotland divided into two camps. The argument was over the patronage exercised by the lairds or principal landowners, whose prerogative it was to appoint the Minister for the parish rather than allowing the parishioners to make their own choice. The second Marquis of Breadalbane, sympathising with those opposed to patronage, actively supported the break away from the Church of Scotland and in the Parish of Kilbrandon and Kilchattan provided land and money to build a Free Church near the Balvicar Crossroads. Now a private house, its cruciform structure and tall windows leave the passer-by in no doubt as to its origins.

Towards the end of the 19th century the dwindling band of

Covenanters in the district began to realise that they had no future unless they joined with another church. Nearest to themselves in religious practices were the members of the Free Church of Scotland and in 1900 the two congregations combined to form the United Free Church. In order to show that both groups were occupying level ground, they sold off former church property and purchased a prefabricated, iron clad church building which was erected on Smithy Brae a few hundred yards north of the Kilbride Township.

Once again there were three church communities in the district. On the death of the second Marquis of Breadalbane in 1864, the third Marquis, a devout member of the Church of Scotland, redressed the balance by presenting the parishioners with a new church building, the present Kilbrandon Church on the Cuan Road which was consecrated in 1866. Of the two smaller parish churches, the North Church continued to serve the congregation at the Kilninver end of the parish but the Cuan Church was put up for sale.

Although the third Marquis undoubtedly provided the bulk of the money for this new church building, the parishioners would have been expected to make their own contribution. The 1860s was a decade of great prosperity in the quarries, with 7 million slates a year being exported to outposts of the British Empire all around the globe. It is not hard to imagine the entertainments entered into by the Easdale residents in order to raise the additional money required for the new church. Soirées, concerts, balls and sales of work are frequently mentioned in the *Oban Times* of the period. Unlike their stricter neighbours belonging either to the Free Church of Scotland or the Covenanters, members of the Church of Scotland were not averse to

United Free Church building (1900) on Smiddy Brae

letting their hair down even to the extent of imbibing a few drams in a good cause!

In 1929, with its congregation reduced to a handful of people, the United Free Church joined the Church of Scotland. Their corrugated iron building on Smiddy Brae was abandoned and lay empty for a very long time. Still in the ownership of the Kilbride Farm, its likely fate is utilisation as a farm building to house livestock.

In 1932, the South and North Churches were united and the North Church was sold off for private housing.

The Breadalbane connection with Kilbrandon Church ended with the breaking up of the Breadalbane estates and the death of the Marchioness in the 1930s. A set of stained glass windows commemorating her life was commissioned and presented to the church by Miss Catherine McKinnon in 1938. The windows, remarkable for the predominance of blue and green colouring, depict aspects of Christ's life beside and upon the sea and are the work of Dr Douglas Strachan.

In May 1996, 130 years after its consecration, a special service was held in the church to commemorate reconstruction work, recently completed. For these improvements, the parish was obliged to raise the sum of £60,000. £13,000 came from the sale of the old Manse at Ellenabeich (now Atlantic House). £10,550 came from grants awarded by the Church of Scotland, The Baird Trust and Strathclyde Regional Council. The remaining £19,500 was raised from individual donations and fund raising events in the parish.

Although, as elsewhere in the country, the regular congregation today represents but a small percentage of residents in the parish, at times of great happiness or great distress, it is to the church that the people go to demonstrate their community spirit. For weddings and funerals it is common to find folk crowding into the old wooden pews, sitting on the steps of the pulpit and standing in the aisles.

Remote though the parish may be, the church does not look backwards. In 1998 the first woman Minister, Freda Marshall, was appointed, bringing with her a refreshing outlook and a buoyant spirit.

The two remaining churches of Kilbrandon and Kilchattan, both serviced by the same minister, provide a centre of community activity on the islands, taking a very positive role in the life of the schools and providing a social as well as a spiritual focus for the people of Netherlorn.

CHAPTER 7

Communications

FOR CENTURIES THE MOST convenient means of travel to the west coast of Scotland was by sea. By the mid-19th century large numbers of tourists as well as residents and itinerant workers travelled to the Slate Islands by steamer.

A steamer in busy Easdale harbour

The slate upon which the Easdale people depended for their livelihood was also transported by sea. Local slate boats would tie up inside Easdale harbour, at Blackmill Bay on Luing or in Balvicar Bay, but the larger ocean going vessels anchored in the sheltered Easdale Sound and were loaded from small boats plying to and from the islands. In 1825, the year that the post office was established at Kilninver, the ships using Easdale harbour amounted to 7 brigs, 15 schooners, 5 galliots, 254 sloops and 245 steamboats. The *New Statistical Account* refers to this period:

> Here might be seen the engineer of the work, John Whyte, plying his little bark across the Sound, propelled by the Archimedes screw. This ingenious piece of mechanism was his own invention ...

The system John Whyte employed is one which is used for ferries to this day. A chain lies on the river or seabed. The vessel is attached to this by a flexible rod or chain and to a system of cog wheels which reduce the force required. By the turning of a handle, the boat can be moved back and forth across the water without other means of propulsion.

Passenger steamers tied up at the steamship pier which was erected outside the main quarry at Ellenabeich. The pier is now in danger of complete collapse. In recent times surveys have been made with a view to reconstructing it and also demolishing it. Like so many projects devised to improve the facilities and appearance of the area, neither proposition ever left the drawing board. In the 1990s however, money was found to restore the old piers and slip-ways on either side of Easdale Sound and the result is a visually pleasing and practical reconstruction suited to the present day requirements of the islanders. Similarly, the ferry waiting room on Easdale Island was given a facelift in 1997. Proposals have been put forward to replace the old waiting room on Ellenabeich pier which was blown away by the January storms of 1998.

In the mid-19th century it was possible to board the steamer at Easdale pier in mid morning and, arriving at Crinan at two o'clock in the afternoon, sail in the narrow canal boat, the *Linnet*, across the Kintyre peninsular to Ardrishaig on Loch Fyne. Here one would board a Clyde steamer, which arrived at Broomielaw Quay, Glasgow, in time to catch the London train that same evening.

For local journeys overland, a horse-drawn open carriage was often used but passengers could expect to get out and walk on the steeper slopes. Even when the internal combustion engine took over in the 1930s, there was an unwritten rule about who would dismount from the omnibus at the foot of Kilninver Brae to help push, and who would be allowed to ride up the hill.

There are many instances of people walking great distances, either to the towns and cities or to the principal Estate Office at Taymouth Castle. The Easdale Volunteers are recorded in Queen Victoria's *Journal* as having walked to Taymouth Castle when Her Majesty was the guest of the Earl of Breadalbane in 1842.

Dr Patrick Gillies's family recall accounts of his walking from Easdale to Glasgow when he was a student. This is not so extra-ordinary as one might think. If a straight line is drawn across country from Loch Feochan through Scammadale Pass to Loch Fyne, over the pass to Loch Long and Loch Lomond, the present day mileage from Easdale to Glasgow is very much reduced. It should be remembered that in those days it was possible to find a boat to ferry you across from almost any village along the loch shore.

Following the completion of the rail link between Oban and Glasgow in the 1890s, islanders began to travel more regularly to Oban, fast developing into a busy port and holiday centre. Initially their only means of travel was on foot or horseback, but when a properly metalled road was eventually constructed linking Easdale across Seil island to the main Oban road, a local entrepreneur started the Easdale Omnibus Company, making possible a weekly shopping expedition into town.

Prior to this there had been little incentive for those living on the Slate Islands to travel to Oban. The 1861 census shows us that before the coming of the railway, Oban was a fishing port whose population was about 600. In the same year, the combined parishes of Kilbrandon and Kilchattan, which included the islands of Seil, Easdale and Luing, supported a population of 3,000.

In the final decades of the 19th century, the telephone brought instant communication with the outside world. A report in the *Oban Times* of 16 March 1878 tells of the excitement created by the installation of the first telephone in Ellenabeich village:

> On several occasions during the week Mr McLean, the recently appointed postmaster of Oban, has afforded some of the residents here the rare treat of speaking and hearing by means of this wonderful instrument. Arrangements having been made with Mr Cowan, the local postmaster, the opportunity was eagerly taken of holding converse with parties in Oban, sixteen miles distant ...

A hundred years ago the district, being known collectively as Easdale, had its own postmark, and there were several collections daily. A letter sent from Easdale would reach its destination in London next day. A reply could be expected within three days. Now there is one delivery and one collection, on weekdays only.

A postal service was established at Kilninver in 1825 and later a post office was opened in Ellenabeich village. From an early date there was a sub post office on Easdale Island. Others were soon established at Achfolla on Luing, at Clachan Seil and at Balvicar. The sub post office on Easdale Island continued in existence until it was finally closed down on 31 October 1959, while that at Clachan Seil closed in the late 1980s. The other offices remain in operation to this day.

While quarries were all operating on the Slate Islands, there was a constant communication between the industrial representatives themselves and the workforce who moved around the district from quarry to quarry as the work became available. Arrangements were in place for a postal service between Easdale, Balvicar and Achfolla as early as 1838. Mail was carried at first on foot around the parish, but on horseback across country to Glasgow. With the coming of the steam passenger boat service, post was carried to Inverness, Fort William and Glasgow by sea, Blackmill Bay Post Office becoming the main sorting office at the time. A post bus now runs daily between Easdale and Luing providing a passenger service as well as making regular deliveries to the inhabitants on Luing.

Towards the end of the 19th century, a slate quarry was opened up on the island of Belnahua. This was an island which had never been in the ownership of the Breadalbanes so the proprietors operated in isolation from the other slate quarries in the district. Once a village had been established and a permanent population had moved in, some means of regular communication was essential. A weekly postal service, from Cullipool on Luing to the island of Belnahua, was established in 1898.

CHAPTER 8

Food, Agriculture and Wildlife

IN THE EARLIEST TIMES the inhabitants of the Slate Islands depended upon the sea for their food. What they caught was augmented by grain crops, grown on the more fertile islands of Luing and Seil, and hedgerow fruits in season. Sheep and a few cows, kept principally for milking, provided an additional occasional source of protein.

As the number of quarrymen employed throughout the area increased, the problem of provisioning the workers and their families must have been a source of anxiety to the owners. Access to the villages by road was difficult. Supplies could be shipped in by the slate boats on their return journeys, but the time taken for such voyages meant that fresh fruit and vegetables were a rarity. The employers encouraged their people to grow their own root vegetables by allocating areas of ground for gardens. This was not a problem on Luing and Seil islands where there was some depth of soil and a number of well sheltered glens for cultivation. On Easdale Island and in Ellenabeich village, however, because the soil is only inches deep and consists mainly of powdered slate with little humus, the slate boats returning from Ireland began to bring in soil as ballast. This was spread on the garden plots, each of which was surrounded by a protective wall of slate rock.

The main vegetable crop produced in the gardens was the potato. In addition, cabbages, spinach and turnips could be grown, although carrots fared badly in the rough stony soil. Salad vegetables were virtually unknown until the later years of the 19th century when summer visitors began to demand them. By this time, the daily steamer run was available to bring fresh produce from the Glasgow markets.

The people of Ellenabeich have to cross the village street to reach their gardens while the sites of those on Easdale Island are clearly visible from the hill even today. They form a patchwork of wall-enclosed plots whose dense undergrowth indicates where the soil is fertile. Easdale brambles are renowned throughout the district and bring to the island every September an army of visitors bent on gathering the fruit for jams and pie fillings, just as their ancestors must have done a hundred years ago.

In the 1930s Col. Arthur Murray purchased a row of derelict cottages which included the Easdale Distillery, close to the Inshaig Park Hotel. He converted the cottages to a substantial dwelling house and with his wife, the actress Faith Celli, created the garden of An Cala on the rough stony hillside. Today An Cala is recognised as one of the best small gardens in Scotland.

The sea provided the bulk of dietary protein for the slate quarriers and their families. White fish was cured and smoked. Herring were pickled in brine. A cod's head was considered a great delicacy. Salmon was plentiful, so much so that it was considered to be poor man's fare and quite unsuitable for the laird's table. One island resident recalls her embarrassment if, as a schoolgirl, she was given salmon sandwiches for her piece (sandwich). More affluent children would not even consider swapping with her!

A large variety of shellfish was also available. Oysters, mussels, lobsters, prawns and scallops were used for soups and fillings. In very hard times even limpets found their way to the table.

Seaweed offered an additional source of nourishment, the most favoured variety being Carragheen or Iceland Moss. This, when boiled, became a gelatinous mess rich in protein and easily swallowed. It was particularly useful for feeding infants and the sick and elderly.

Today, in the sheltered waters of Balvicar Sound, oysters are reared. Local fishermen rely upon onshore catches of fine shellfish, crabs, prawns, lobsters and in happier days, scallops, providing a lucrative haul. These waters were at one time well stocked with wild salmon but unfortunately the fish was netted nearly to extinction during the 1970s and 1980s.

For the most part, the shores around the Slate Islands have escaped the worst exigencies of the fish farming explosion which took place in so many locations along the west coast of Scotland during the final decade of the 20th century. With proposals to designate the reefs in the Firth of Lorn as Sites of Special Scientific Interest, it is to be hoped that there will be a restriction upon any further developments which might harm the natural environment of these waters.

On Seil and Luing, many families kept a cow to provide milk which, together with milk from goats and sheep, was used to make a variety of cheeses as well as butter. Crowdie (curds and whey) formed an excellent food for infants and invalids. On Easdale Island it is probable that one family maintained sufficient milch cows in the mid-19th century to provide for the large number of inhabitants.

In the 19th century, meat was relatively scarce and came almost certainly from older animals. Cows were slaughtered only when their milking days were done. There was insufficient grass to graze beef cattle so that the calves were sold on to cattle farmers in more fertile areas of Argyll. Sheep were shorn many times before they became mutton chops. On rare occasions when there was cause for celebration, the birth of a Breadalbane heir or the accession of a monarch for example, the Marquis would order venison from his vast estates to be distributed to the workmen's families.

Every part of the animal was used. The best of the meat was soaked in brine and smoked in the kitchen chimney. The remainder was salted down for later use. The liver, kidney, brains and heart had to be used immediately, providing a very special treat. Blood was collected and boiled to make black pudding, a dark sausage with a skin made from the animal's intestines. When times were very hard it was not uncommon for a living milch cow to be bled for this purpose. Trouble arose if the beast chosen happened to belong to a neighbour!

Traditional Recipe for Haggis dating from 1856

1 cleaned sheep's or lamb's stomach bag
2lb. dry oatmeal
1lb. chopped mutton suet
1lb. lambs or deer's liver (boiled and minced)
1pt. (2 cups) stock
heart and lights of sheep (boiled and minced)
1 large chopped onion
half teaspoon each of: cayenne pepper, Jamaica pepper, salt and
pepper.
METHOD
Toast the oatmeal slowly until it is crisp. Mix all the ingredients
together (except the stomach bag) and add the stock. Fill the bag
to just over half full, press out the air and sew up securely. Have
ready a large pot full of boiling water. Prick the haggis all over
with a large needle so that it does not burst and boil slowly for 4
to 5 hrs.
Serve with Clapshot and the traditional glass of neat whisky.

Even on Easdale Island cattle roamed the meadow to the west
of the island, while a few sheep were grazed on the hill. A larger
flock of sheep was kept on the uninhabited island of Inish a mile
or two to the north. Recently a letter was received from an elderly
man who had spent his boyhood there, recalling how, at the end
of every summer, island lads were employed to round up the Inish
sheep and get them on to rowing boats to be taken to market on
the mainland.

In recent years there have been several experiments with livestock on Easdale Island. Chickens, bullocks, goats, donkeys and
horses have roamed the waste ground in turn. While the animals
were useful in keeping down the vegetation, their preference was for
the cultivated goodies in the residents' gardens and the wrangling
that ensued between neighbours meant that none of the animals
remained for long. Domestic cats control the population of wild
birds and field voles, the only mammal found on Easdale apart from
visiting seals and otters. The island dogs, able to roam in safety in
the absence of roads and vehicular traffic, consider themselves

agents for tourism, adopting groups of visitors as they disembark the ferry and escorting them on their walks around the island.

On Seil, extensive herds of beef cattle roam the lower meadows and sheep graze the hillsides. In the 1890s it was the Gillies family of doctors who occupied Dunmore House on Seil and farmed the glen. They won many prizes for their beef stock at the local shows. Today the proprietors concentrate on sheep and the rearing of game birds.

On the lush pastures of Luing, the world-renowned, chocolate-coloured Luing cattle are bred and reared by the Cadzow family.

Throughout the 19th century a meal made from oats or barley was the staple food. It was sold by the boll (8kg). In times of unemployment when the quarries were at a standstill, the poorest families were allocated a boll of meal by the Parish Council. This would be augmented by whatever the family could catch at sea or gather from the land until such time as work became available.

Until the 1890s meal was provided from local mills or imported from Ireland. At the end of the 19th century, white flour was being imported from the south and the housewife's baking became more sophisticated. The presence of white scones on any tea table was a mark of affluence and respectability.

In each of the quarrying villages the company store provided dry goods and household necessities for those who were in work and could afford to pay. Because they were paid so infrequently, the men were allowed to accrue debts which were paid off on the settlement day.

Apart from the general grocery store, over the years various residents set up small businesses in the villages. In Ellenabeich there was for a time a bootmaker and a bakery. In 1965 Miss Annabel Parker, a resident on Easdale Island, hoping to produce shortbread to her own special recipe for sale to the general public, was obliged to obtain a licence from the Department of Public Health. Her enterprise required the installation of piped water to her house and an approved form of drainage. Annabel's was the first house on the island to have a septic tank and an indoor bathroom with water closet.

When the company store closed just before the Great War, other premises in succession took on the role of the village shop. As recently as 1988 there was a general grocery store on Easdale Island as well as shops at Ellenabeich, Cullipool and Balvicar, but sadly the coming of the large supermarkets in Oban and the proliferation of private transport to get there have diminished the need for the local shop. Today, not only has the tiny Easdale Island store closed, but also the Ellenabeich village shop has been obliged to cease trading during the winter months. To date, both Luing and Seil have managed to retain one small general store apiece, although the long term prognosis for these fragile businesses is not good.

On the islands of Easdale and Belnahua where farming and horticultural possibilities are limited or non existent and where cattle and sheep are absent, the meadows are left to the only indigenous mammal on these small islands, a tiny field vole. Otters rear their young along the coast and can be seen occasionally on the islands and in the Sound, while seals visit the sea-filled quarries fishing for ling, saithe and cod which become trapped by the falling tide. On Easdale there is a huge population of toads feeding off the slugs and snails so abhorred by gardeners, while sea birds regularly nest on the cliffs and in the wilder areas surrounding the quarries and other uninhabited parts. The larger islands abound with wildlife of all kinds. Badgers, weasels and stoats may be seen roving the hillsides, while rabbits and hedgehogs sadly fall victim to passing traffic, providing a well-stocked larder of carrion for the hooded crows and the buzzards which haunt the valleys as the year draws to a close.

Migrant birds are a constant source of interest to ornithologists, marking the passage of the seasons by their appearances and disappearances. Oyster-catchers herald the coming of the spring, followed swiftly by the spirited little pied-wagtail who struts before the houses, while ringed plover and eider duck populate the shore line. Green-finches, chaffinches, blue-tits, coal-tits and the bluey-grey dunnock appear at the bird tables throughout April, May and June and armies of young hedge sparrows share bare branches and high wires with swallows on their way southwards at the end of July. When they are gone, their place is taken by huge flocks of starlings which descend suddenly upon the islands in the autumn, stay for a short while and then, just as suddenly, disappear. A charm of goldfinches settling in one's garden towards the end of the year is a sight to brighten the dismal prospect of the advance of winter.

Throughout the summer months blackbirds and thrushes feed off the plethora of slugs, snails and leatherjackets which invade our gardens to consume plants which we have studiously protected from gales and salt spray during the winter. On summer evenings the linnets and the tiny wrens trill and seep seep amongst the dense undergrowth of wild fuchsia and blackthorn. As evening falls, along the coast the cormorants fly back and forth between their feeding grounds and their roosts on the rocks and skerries to the north and west – sharp triangles of rock which lie blackly against the orange and ruby sunset sky.

As the days begin to shorten, the fieldfare sings from the topmost branches of the only real tree on Easdale Island, an ancient rowan which grows at the head of the harbour. High above the hills of Seil and Luing, sparrow hawks and buzzards hover in the hope of spotting some tasty morsel, while small fish are always at risk from herons who stake their claim to stretches of loch shore, the harbours and sea-filled quarries in the early hours of the morning. At least one of these has an expensive taste in goldfish, as one keen aquatic gardener has discovered to his cost.

The islands support a flora which includes several unique varieties of coastal species as well as a profusion of more common wild flowers. Since the quarries ceased working and many filled with water, the waste slate has been gradually inundated by the growth of lichens, mosses and tiny alpine plants such as the wild thyme and stone crop. Grasses and taller perennial flowering plants have followed, angelica and wild carrot, pig nut and sea plantain poke their heavy heads above a sea of waving grasses. Heathers have invaded the rim of the quarries and together with the gently waving harebell are reflected in the still clear waters on a summer's day. Rusting pipework and old boilers provide a bright splash of colour in the dense green of the undergrowth, and derelict stone buildings softened by creeping vines provide a romantic framework to this extraordinary wilderness.

As you wander in the wild areas of these beautiful islands, step lightly on the growing plants, particularly where they have inhabited the waste slate lying loosely over the surface. It has taken a hundred years to attain the growth which now softens and disguises the man-made scars of an obsolete industry. Years of effort may be undone by one careless footfall or the thoughtless uprooting of a single plant.

CHAPTER 9

Growing up in the Slate Islands

FROM THE TIME OF the formation of the Marble and Slate Quarrying Company of Netherlorn in 1745, quarrymen and their families began to take up permanent residence first on Easdale Island and later on Seil and Luing. Easdale, lacking as it did a supply of fresh water, other than what could be collected in water butts and natural pools, was not a promising site for a large settlement. The narrow channel between Easdale and Seil could be rough, and in any case, travel across country was arduous and sometimes dangerous. The most important means of communication with the outside world was the sea itself and thus it was that the children born on the islands learned early to respect the sea around them, to handle the multitude of small boats which plied to and from the various villages in the vicinity and to collect whatever came ashore which was either edible or useful.

In the early days when women and children were employed to carry waste slate and made slates across the island either in hand carts or in creels strapped to their backs, there was little time for play and even less for schooling.

Once the transportation of the slate became mechanised, there was no longer any need to employ child labour. It was now possible for the lowest classes of society to send their children to school, provided they could afford the few pennies charged for tuition.

Prior to the passing of the 1870 Education Act, parishes were not compelled to provide schooling, although many did. Teaching was sometimes undertaken by the Church or by private individuals who scraped a living from the very small tuition fees which could be charged. The school room might be in the Manse or in a private house. Rarely was there a building especially designed for the purpose.

School at Ellenabeich, 1890s

In the case of the quarrying community at Easdale, it was the Slate Quarrying Company which provided schoolmasters and school buildings both on Easdale Island and in the village of Ellenabeich. The standard of these schools in the 18th century was very variable. One school, held in the Manse of the Free Church at Kilbride Township on Smithy Brae, produced a most famous pupil, John McLachlan, who became Chaplain to Prince Charles Edward Stuart during the 1745 Uprising. On the other hand, a letter addressed to His Lordship, The Marquis of Breadalbane, in 1790, states:

> I believe there is nowhere in Scotland so miserable a hovel as a Parochial Schoolhouse, as this on Seil ...

The location of this particular school is not known but is likely to have been at Oban Seil on Seil Island.

A written account of an Easdale school in the mid-19th century tells us that there was no wooden floor in the schoolroom, only bare slate slabs. There was a small fire which was kept going by each of the children bringing a piece of coal or a peat to school every morning. A child who forgot, or could not afford his piece of coal, was made to sit furthest from the fire.

At first the children learned to write upon slates, usually man-ufactured by their fathers from material found in the quarries. The slate was smoothed by rubbing with sand and water to provide a flat surface, and set in a crude wooden frame. Slate pencils were hard to come by, but the writer recalls a large boulder, situated near Balvicar, which was particularly useful for this purpose. Children would be sent off with a hammer and chisel to cut out a suitably sized chunk from the rock.

When the children progressed to using pens, these were made from goose quills. Even by the 1860s when steel pens were readily available, they were considered too expensive for use by quarriers' children. Cutting and trimming the quills took up quite a lot of the teacher's time, while the provision of ink, using a powder that must be mixed with water, was a messy job reserved as a punish-ment for backward pupils.

Transgressions were dealt with by use of the tawse, a multi-thonged strip of leather bound onto a short wooden handle. Generally punishment was received on the hands, but some schoolmasters were no too particular which part of the anatomy they chose to attack.

When in the 1840s John Campbell, the fifth Earl and second Marquis of Breadalbane, bought out his co-directors and set about running the quarries himself, he provided proper schools for the quarry worker's children. Four schools are recorded as function-ing in the district between 1843 and 1845: the Easdale Island School, the Ellenabeich School which was housed in the Old Distillery (one of the cottages which now makes up the house at An Carla, next door to the present school), one beside the Clachan Bridge and the other at Barnacarry. The school at Clachan Farm is thought to have existed for 600 years. The Chief of Clan McDonald is said to have been educated here at the time of Robert the Bruce.

At Ellenabeich, a purpose-built school was opened in 1877. The same building, much improved and extended, is still in use today. When, towards the end of the 19th century, quarries were opened at Cullipool and Toberonochy and the number of quarrymen's families grew, an additional local authority-maintained school was opened on Luing to accommodate the influx of children.

On Easdale Island there were several small schools at different times during the 19th century, but a proper schoolhouse was built at much the same period as the Ellenabeich school. Today this is a private house. Careful examination reveals that the tall windows, placed high up to prevent the children seeing out while they were learning, have been only partly disguised. The house has two storeys with remarkably high ceilings for an Easdale construction.

In the log books of Easdale Public School (Ellenabeich), reference is made to the existence of an Easdale Island side school as late as the mid 1940s when it must have been closed due to lack of pupils. The roll had been reduced to six children in 1938 when the only families with children of school age on the island were those of the brothers McQueen, boatbuilders. It is said that when an inspector came to address the children he called upon McQueen to answer and every child in the classroom stood up!

A report of His Majesty's Inspector dated 19th April 1931 states:

> This is a very well taught and pleasant little school. The children are bright and happy and their progress is distinctly good.

On 22 August 1933, Easdale Island side school (number on roll 9) was amalgamated with the Easdale Public School at Ellenabeich (number on roll 20). The combined schools did not warrant a two teacher school. Miss McFarlane, who was the teacher for the island school, was dismissed, as was the assistant teacher at Ellenabeich.

One can only surmise the action which was then taken by the School Board as a result of their treatment at the insensitive hands of the Argyll Education Department. Suffice it to say that on 16 October, only eight weeks later, the Easdale Island School was re-opened and Miss McFarlane reinstated. Mr Macintosh, the Headmaster of Easdale Public School, who was threatened with a reduction in his salary when the school was demoted, found work elsewhere and his place as taken by a Miss Sarah McDonald of Jura School. She took over a roll of 20 pupils.

Easdale Island side school appears to have been largely independent of the Ellenabeich school although the Head Teacher visited the island for an official inspection twice a year. HMIS continued to be satisfied with the pupils' progress as a report of 24 April 1935 suggests:

Easdale Island School:
The present teacher who has just taken up duty in this school is fortunate in finding it in a high state of efficiency. The children are most pleasingly responsive and well advanced in every branch of the instruction.

There appears to have been some lack of communication within the Inspectorate, for in his comments upon this report the Director for Education in Argyll excuses a poor showing at the Ellenabeich school on the grounds that the new teacher, Miss MacDonald, had only recently taken over a less than satisfactory situation whereas the Easdale Island side school was fortunate in having had the same teacher, Miss McFarlane, for seven years with the exception of a short period during 1933, when the school had been closed.

When the island school was eventually closed, early in the 1940s, the few children left attended school on Seil Island. At that time the ferry was a rowing boat which could neither tackle the sea at all states of the tide nor in bad weather. The school log records frequent absences of Easdale Island children because they could not cross the sea to school. Despite this, Jean McQueen, frequently listed as an absentee, won a bursary to Oban High School. One wonders if the teacher dismissed when Easdale Island side school closed was not still on hand to help the island pupils.

Since the children were by this time crossing daily on the ferry, it is not surprising to find that as they grew strong enough, they were allowed to take an oar to assist the ferryman. Some of the older islanders claim that they learned to row by taking the ferry across the water to the school.

Once the quarries closed in 1911, the numbers enrolled at the Ellenabeich School fluctuated according to the prosperity of the islands. At the beginning of the Great War, there were 50 pupils but by the 1930s the number was down to 18, with never more than 10 pupils attending the Easdale Island side school.

By the outbreak of the Second World War there were 9 local pupils and 8 evacuees. Those evacuated from Glasgow and Dunoon frequently disappeared for weeks at a time and the roll constantly fluctuated between 9 and 20 pupils. This must have been a constant source of concern to the single remaining teacher, wondering at what point the Education Department would decide to close the school. The difficulty of the situation is illustrated by some poignant entries made by a Mrs McDougal in November 1943. Falling ill herself, the lady applied to the Education Office for a stand-in. No temporary teacher being available, Mrs McDougal reports that next day she returned to duty. Resuming school following the Christmas holiday, she was obliged to hold classes in her own living room because of the poor operation of the heating system in the school.

Frequent absences of Easdale Island children are reported during the winter of 1945, a Mr McQueen having refused to allow his children to cross the Channel during bad weather. As a protest and no doubt hoping to reinstate the island school, he withdrew his children from the school from January until April. Unfortunately his protest had no effect upon the Local Authority.

For a while, following the end of the war in 1945, the numbers on the roll rose, but as returning ex-servicemen failed to find employment, more and more families left the district, often taking up attractive emigration schemes offered by the colonies.

The school roll fell once again and hovered between 6 and 10 pupils until, on the night of 29 November 1956, Ardencapel School was burnt to the ground. Next day the Easdale Public School roll had risen by 24 to a total of 30 pupils. Although a small school was rebuilt at Ardencapel for children in the immediate vicinity, those who lived at Balvicar were now transferred permanently to Easdale and a bus was provided to carry them back and forth.

When the Ardencapel school eventually closed, all the children on Seil Island were collected by bus and delivered to the Ellenabeich school, never again to come under the threat of closure.

Today's school population is in most years between 50 and 60. To ensure that no valuable lesson time is lost, the Headmistress has contingency plans for occupying the Easdale Island children at home when the crossing is too rough for them to attend school. The introduction of motor powered ferry boats with successively more efficient engines has made crossing the Sound, even in the worst weather, a more realistic proposition. All the children must be equipped with life jackets which they wear most conscientiously. The occasions when children cannot get to school are quite rare.

On Luing at the turn of the century, there were small infant schools in the main villages of Cullipool and Toberonochy but the main school, attended by all the children until they left to go to work or on to Oban High School, was at Achafolla in the centre of the island. Built at the same time as the Easdale School, today Luing Primary School has around twenty children on roll each year.

Following the introduction of the 1870 Education Act, the schools were made the responsibility of the Parish Council and came under the supervision of the local Minister who inspected progress from time to time and provided religious instruction for the pupils. Administration was by a School Board generally made up of the Factor, representing the Marquis, members of the local gentry, the doctor and the manager of the slate quarries.

The standard achieved by pupils in the latter part of the 19th century was impressive. The majority of children left school at the age of 11 able to read, write and calculate. For those willing to stay on until they were 13, the curriculum extended beyond the three RS, German and French Language, History, Geography and Navigation being on offer as additional subjects. A small charge (1d) was made for ordinary lessons, with an additional fee for the extra subjects.

On leaving school, most of the boys went into the quarries, the brighter ones attending classes in mathematics and engineering subjects at the Easdale Technical Institute during the evenings. The Marquis of Breadalbane like so many of his wealthy contemporaries took a philanthropic interest in the welfare of his poorer fellow men. As a member of the Board of Governors of the prestigious George Watson's School in Edinburgh, he was entitled to nominate a number of boys each year to attend the school as Scholarship pupils. This was not entirely altruistic, since by this means the Marquis harnessed to his service the most intelligent and potentially useful young people on his estates. Lawyers, doctors, engineers and factors were educated and retained in this way.

On leaving school, girls went into service locally as housemaids, dairymaids or nannies to the wealthy landowners and the more prosperous tenant farmers. Their ultimate goal was marriage and while it was considered important that wives and mothers should be educated sufficiently to bring up their families wisely and well, there was no suggestion that even the brightest girls should aspire to higher education or any career other than, perhaps, teaching. Towards the end of the 19th century classes were established to teach the older girls skills which would enable them to find work outside the home. Cheesemaking, spinning and weaving classes were held. There is no doubt that many young women owed their skills with the needle to the sewing groups which met socially to provide garments for the poor and needy of the parish.

There was little money which could be spared for toys in Victorian times but examples of simple wooden dolls and carved balls have been discovered in the locality. These can be seen in the Easdale Island Museum. Books were rare, generally of an improving nature and rather dull. A number of religious tracts for children and a few copies of the *Children's Newspaper* have survived.

Nowadays all the primary children on Luing attend school at Achafolla while on Seil and Easdale, they attend school at Ellenabeich until they are 11, after which they all transfer to Oban High School. Rough weather and limited ferry hours during the winter months make it difficult for the Easdale pupils to travel daily into Oban. Like children from the Outer Isles, they live in a hostel during the week, returning home only at weekends.

CHAPTER 10

People and Pastimes

ALTHOUGH LIFE WAS HARD and money scarce, the quarrying communities never lacked for entertainment. A visit to the Easdale Island Museum will show evidence of the pastimes enjoyed by the quarriers and their families from sailing, fishing and skating to music making, picnicking and cycling. Reference is made to balls and ceilidhs held in the Volunteer's Drill Hall.

From the mid-19th century onwards, adult education was a feature of island life. A Technical Institute was introduced to further the education, initially, of the young boys joining the quarries. Classes were, however, attended by all ages and lectures were given by the Quarry Master, the Doctor, the Minister ... whoever could put himself forward as an expert in some subject of interest to all. At a time when the quarries were at peak production, the philanthropist Sir Peter Coates of Paisley donated a library of books to the Easdale Technical Institute. This must have been a tremendous encouragement to the men at a time when technical information was at a premium and books very expensive.

Social life centred for the most part around the various churches in the Parish. A Women's Guild, several Friendly Societies and the Easdale Volunteer Company (forerunner of the Territorial Army) not only performed their specific functions in the community, but by their fundraising activities provided a focus for entertainment of every kind. Sales of work, soirées, musical concerts, whist drives were regularly reported in the *Oban Times*.

The Friendly Societies were mainly temperance groups set up to counter the demon drink. By means of small weekly contributions from members, they also provided insurance against sickness and contributed towards funeral expenses. In the early days of the National Health Insurance Scheme which was introduced by

Lloyd George in 1911, it was bodies such as these which were used as the organs for administering the funds.

During the summer months the quarrymen and their families engaged in sporting activities. Highland Games were held every year in the grounds of Dunmore House, just as they are to this day, and one can imagine that the burly slate workers would make light of tossing a caber or hurling a stone. The men, being skilful seamen, were very successful in the annual regattas which took place up and down the coast. They were renowned throughout the Highlands for their splendid oarsmanship and it was hardly surprising that the Marquis of Breadalbane should call upon them when he needed a team of bargemen for a very special purpose.

In the early 1840s the young Queen Victoria and her Consort had purchased an estate at Balmoral and began their annual pilgrimage to the Highlands. At this time there was no railway north of Edinburgh, and the journey by road involved taking a circuitous route inland to find a convenient crossing of the River Tay.

When she visited Balmoral in 1842, Victoria was invited to

Some Easdale quarriers training for the next regatta

63

break her long journey north by staying at the Breadalbane family seat, Taymouth Castle near Aberfeldy.

The Marquis, anxious to show off the beauties of his vast estates to best advantage, decided that part of her itinerary should include a sixteen-mile journey by boat along Loch Tay to his cottage of Auchmore at the head of the loch. Insisting that no less than the most expert of boatmen on his estates should be chosen to row the Monarch, he called upon the Easdale men.

Lead by Pipe Major John McPherson, his plaid fastened with the famous Brooch of Lorn, twenty quarrymen wearing full Highland dress in the Campbell of Breadalbane tartan, made the three days march from Easdale to Aberfeldy to attend their Queen.

In her *Leaves from the Journal of Our Lives in the Highlands*, Queen Victoria recorded the incident thus:

> The boatmen sang two Gaelic boat songs, very wild and singular, the language so guttural and yet so soft. Captain McDougal, who steered and who is the head of the McDougals, showed us the real Brooch of Lorn which was taken by his ancestor, from Robert the Bruce, in battle. One of the songs sung by an Easdale man was what is known as Tuireadh bean Mhic-aan-t-saoir which begins A nighean ud thall Tug O.

John McPherson was over six feet in height and a very imposing figure. When, in 1860, the second Marquis raised the Easdale Company of Artillery Volunteers, John was chosen as Right Hand Man, the senior NCO of the battery. John died at Easdale in 1906 at the age of 86.

Although Victorian society frowned upon the excessive consumption of alcohol, there was always a regular source of supply of the uisge beatha. In mid-century this would have been the distillery which was sited in a cottage forming a part of what is now known as An Cala House. The burn running through the famous gardens and down to the sea appears on Ordnance Survey maps as the Distillery Burn. The only inn in the village for decades was a temperance hotel. When the Quarry Manager's house was purchased and turned into a licensed house, The Inshaig Park Hotel, the schoolmaster, Mr Stewart, proposed a toast to the success of the new owners, a Mrs Gillies and her son. This prompted a spate of correspondence in the *Oban Times* under the heading, 'Whisky and Education' at Easdale:

Oban Times, 24 December 1887

... we have, through your columns, read a good deal regarding the small wages earned by the Easdale quarriers and the consequent impoverished conditions of many of them. Yet, in the face of this, we find a grand hotel with more than the ordinary facilities for dram drinking; opened to lure these quarriers from their hard earned wages. This alone might grieve anyone who took the slightest interest in the people of Easdale, but a more painful fact is contained in the statement that the leading man at the opening ceremony was the teacher of the Public School. Instead of finding him, as all true friends of education would naturally expect, protesting against a public house being opened next door to his school, he is found proposing the toast of 'PROSPERITY' to an institution which is the bitter foe of true education and the fruitful parent of ignorance and vice. Growing bolder as the hours stole on, this educationalist took upon himself to reply for the Earl of Breadalbane, who erected the hotel, while later on he distinguished himself by proposing the toast of ' THE PRESS'. Such are some of the painful features of the report and were it not for the fact that all the persons who are mentioned as having graced the feast - with the exception of one, the Contractors, are aliens and not natives to the district, one would be inclined to mourn in sack-cloth and ashes ...

signed X.Y.Z.

There was occasional excitement engendered by political events. The Breadalbanes who had always been Whigs, now supported the Liberal Party. The quarrymen traditionally followed the Marquis' lead in all things, despite the fact that they were by now employees of tenants and not the Marquis himself. At a meeting held on 14 May 1887, they voted in support of Home Rule for Scotland and Ireland.

Oban Times, 23 July 1892

Easdale: The result of the election was received here with a great deal of satisfaction by a large crowd which assembled outside the Post Office shortly after 12 o'clock on Thursday morning. Cheer after cheer was raised for Mr McFarlane and for Mr Gladstone. Mr Neil MacDougall, who had acted as Mr McFarlane's polling agent at Cullipool, was carried shoulder high amidst the greatest enthusiasm. Two volleys were fired from the cannons on the Dun to warn the people of Luing of the good news. On Thursday night large bonfires were seen to be blazing on the highest hill in Luing and on the Dun at Easdale. It may be mentioned that the farmers' and quarriers' vote in this district went almost solid for Mr McFarlane.

McFarlane was the Liberal MP for the district. His etched portrait appeared in the newspaper that week, one of the first blocks ever printed in the *Oban Times*. A Liberal Member represents the Parliamentary constituency to this day.

A VOTES FOR WOMEN badge, found in one of the cottages, suggests that at least one of the island's female population supported the Movement for Women's Suffrage.

A hundred years on, the centres for island activity are the Tigh an Truish and Inshaig Park Hotels and the Puffer Bar on Easdale Island together with the community halls (once the Volunteers Drill Halls, on Seil and Easdale). On Luing there is a campaign to build a new community centre for the island where, lacking an hotel or pub, for the time being the school and church act as centres for communal activities. Events such as engagements and weddings, Halloween and Hogmanay are celebrated. Islanders meet together when some important matter demands a collective approach from their Community Councils. In summer there are barbecues, while ceilidhs are held throughout the year at the slightest excuse.

In recent years, the Easdale Island Trust has undertaken a large number of events in order to raise funds to restore the old Drill Hall on Easdale Island. Gala days, musical events and sports activities have created a focus of attention, bringing residents of the other Slate Islands and even visitors from Oban to the island. If on occasion such activities are a source of a certain amount of contention between diferent groups on the island, this in itself keeps the adrenaline running and brings people together for collective action.

Of all the Slate Islands, Easdale as a place to live is the most unusual and deserves some special mention.

There is no compulsion for anyone to live on Easdale Island today. Many might shy away from a place where there are neither roads nor paved footpaths, where you walk across the wet grass to get from house to house and where the only means of transport is a wheelbarrow. The island's extraordinary character – charm is hardly the word for a derelict industrial site which has lain fallow for a hundred years – has made Easdale the magnet for a unique body of people whose only reason for living here together is their love of the place. Few spots can provide the tranquillity, scenic beauty and sense of remoteness which are the Slate Island's bonus to mankind, and yet remain within half an hour of the real world of juggernaught lorries and supermarkets.

Every occupation and talent is represented in the islands from workers in wood and slate to university professors and oil-rig engineers. While there is limited opportunity for employment in the villages, Oban is only half an hour away by road and many islanders commute to their work. For some the islands are a haven of rest from their regular work overseas. It is a perfect place for those who work from home, online. There are probably more computers per head of population than anywhere in Scotland!

The islands have always acted as a home base for mariners. The skipper of the last working puffer boat on the Western seaboard lived here until he emigrated to Australia in 1989. A Commodore of the P&O fleet of oil tankers, Graham Bevis, lived here, as did one of our oldest inhabitants during the last decade of the 20th century, Jack Buchanan. A radio officer in the Merchant Navy at the time of the first great Atlantic battle of 1940, Jack was the first to report signals from the damaged German Raider, *Admiral Graff Spee*, as she sailed for sanctuary in Montevideo harbour. On his retirement to Easdale, Jack acted as auxiliary coastguard on the island of Easdale and kept track of vessels passing up and down the Sound of Lorn. Rarely could one visit his house without the accompaniment of Morse code which, even in his eighties, he was able to interpret while holding a conversation about some quite different topic. Sadly, Jack died in January 1998 at the age of 82. He is commemorated by the seat provided for visitors which stands outside the ferry waiting room.

Expertise upon any subject is readily available among the islanders, as those who would seek to disturb the present state of affairs have discovered to their cost. In a recent attempt by a development company to overturn the Argyll and Bute Council's decision to deny planning consent for an experimental cod farm in one of the sea filled quarries on Easdale, the islanders were able to muster the support of 14 witnesses against the proposal, each qualified to give an expert opinion in his or her own sphere.

The islands do not provide, in general, for the future employment of their children, although in recent years there have been a number of craftsmen trained by the various small businesses in building, fish processing and farming. In general the children, having spent their teenage years at Oban High School, continue into Higher Education. No matter where their ambitions lead them, they return to the islands for rest and recuperation, savouring the delights of renewing old acquaintances and recounting stories of their childhood.

The July fortnight and Hogmanay are times when the young come back to the islands, bringing with them their partners from another world. Maybe one day some of them will return to enjoy, on a more permanent basis, the heritage created for them by a small community of people determined to maintain a simple way of life which they value above all things.

CHAPTER 11

What of the Future?

WITH ITS SLATE RESERVES used up and without services of any kind, the island of Belnahua is likely to remain uninhabited, the only indication of its industrial past being the ruined houses, which each year disintegrate a little more, and the discarded machinery, now hidden by waist high grasses. It is a haven for botany and a paradise for the student of wildlife. An aim of the Slate Islands Heritage Trust is to make a complete record of what remains of the village and the slate quarrying operation, but otherwise to leave it in peace.

The islands of Luing and Seil have a strong agricultural background upon which, together with an increasing tourist industry, rests the economy of the island communities. There has been a steady although well controlled increase in housing stocks in recent years and many of the older buildings have received a facelift. One indication that there is cause for optimism about the future population of these islands is the recent opening of a new doctor's surgery, providing the facilities for first class primary health care in the community. An increase in the number of houses providing bed and breakfast and the number of holiday cottages on all the Slate Islands, together with three small but viable hotels all sited on the island of Seil, has created many new opportunities for tourism. The Slate Islands Heritage Trust will endeavour to co-operate with the many other organisations in the district to increase the provision of entertainment and interest for the holiday visitor. Those residents of Seil and Luing who cannot find work in the immediate area commute to Oban and the surrounding country, wherever employment can be found. In this respect the single track B844 is the lifeline of the island people. Improvements to this road are paramount if the area is to continue to develop in the future.

Like so many of Scotland's island paradises, there are many properties, including Easdale island, in the hands of an absentee landlord. What these people choose to do, in absentia, with their particular holdings in the Slate Islands seriously affects the lives of all the inhabitants.

Windmill Quarry at high tide

The quality of life on these islands lies in a delicate balance. An increase in trading activity of any kind would certainly bring greater prosperity to those operations depending upon visitor input, but because of the limited accommodation and the nature of the area's attractions, that increase in numbers could affect the balance between built, cultivated and wild areas, and would destroy the very aspects which are the attraction to living in the islands. To make use of the discarded, water-filled quarries in any way which disturbs their appearance, would be to destroy the tranquillity which is afforded by these vast natural mirrors reflecting the ever changing skies in all their moods. On a fine day the water is so clear that one can see down 70 or 80 metres to the bottom.

The siting of even a single vessel in one of these land-locked pools would destroy that special peace and solitude which is to be found only a five minute stroll outwith the villages. A recent application to site a fish farm in one of the quarries on Easdale Island was strenuously resisted by the islanders and finally turned down after a public enquiry had found that such an enterprise would adversely affect the environment and the fragile economy of the island.

In their concern to preserve the islands as a part of Scotland's industrial heritage, the people have no wish to reconstruct what has decayed beyond repair. It is the wish of the Slate Islands Trust's management committee however, that the industrial buildings be stabilised in their present condition, the sites of historic or natural importance tidied up and properly signed with access for visitors improved. Already a concerted effort has been made to survey many of the industrial buildings to ensure an accurate record of their position, construction and function.

It is felt that there are certain aspects of the islands that must be retained at all costs. Easdale Island has no roads and cannot support heavy vehicular traffic. On Seil and Luing the roads are single track for the most part and some properties are accessible by farm tracks only. This is one aspect of island life which makes it strangely unique at the beginning of the 21st century.

The Slate Islands, despite their designation as a conservation area and a site of outstanding natural beauty, will continue to come under pressure from insensitive developers unless some alternative form of economic improvement can be found which will satisfy the financial aspirations of the owners while leaving, undefiled, the unique character of the area.

So, what can the islands sustain in the way of future development?

There is planning consent for a few more houses. It is to be hoped that when built, these will provide a combination of permanent accommodation for some more young families as well as holiday accommodation to swell the ranks of casual visitors wishing to experience island life for short periods.

The harbours and piers, several long-neglected and threatened

Easdale Harbour

by every great storm, could and should be restored. Such a move would be of benefit to those islanders who depend upon their own boats for both business and pleasure and it would improve conditions for operating the ferry services. Most importantly such improvements would encourage visiting yachts, thereby providing additional income from harbour dues and spending at the various trading facilities.

In addition to the Trust's plans to improve the access to historical sites on the islands, the Easdale Island Heritage Trust, Eilean Eisdeal has been established to acquire funds for the restoration of the Volunteer's Drill Hall on Easdale to provide those islanders with a community hall. This facility will be, among other things, a meeting place for the residents of Easdale and a unique venue for musical and other artistic activities. The additional provision of inexpensive, comfortable, temporary accommodation would encourage the use of the hall for short residential courses in subjects appropriate to the area.

What is patently obvious is that any development must take place slowly so that its impact upon the general character of the islands can be carefully monitored. The economy of the Slate Islands is so fragile that one wet day in summer, a storm which prevents the operation of a ferry, or any occurrence which impairs the ability of island employers to provide tourism services, has a serious effect upon the economy. At present tourism is the sole source of income for many islanders and our first priority must be to minimise the effects of adverse conditions by providing alternative attractions in wet weather and by reducing wherever possible the discomfort experienced by the casual visitor. A ferry to Easdale with access for the disabled, proper public toilet facilities at strategic points throughout the islands and visitor centres at Balvicar and on Luing, providing video shows and exhibitions to augment the work of the Easdale Museum and the Ellenabeich Heritage Centre are all considered in the current proposals.

There is no intention to turn any part of the Slate Islands into a theme park. It has been suggested for instance, that one of the quarries should be pumped dry and set up with models showing the men at work. This is not what is wanted. As has been stated elsewhere, it is enough to provide detailed information of the island's historic past by means of written and spoken word and the Easdale Island Folk Museum and the Slate Islands Heritage Centre already fulfill this function. Little is to be gained by sitting the residents outside their cottage doors, clad in 19th century dress, working their spinning wheels or chipping away at the slates.

The aim of the present day islanders is to preserve what remains of the past, sensitively and discretely, to ensure that any development is not detrimental to the unique nature of the environment and to secure the continued prosperity of the islands by aspiring to greater community control over their future.

The Slate Islands Heritage Trust

The Slate Islands Heritage Trust is committed to the preservation of the heritage of the Slate Islands of Netherlorn: Belnahua, Easdale, Luing and Seil. To this end its aims are to carry out projects recording, preserving and increasing accessibility to places and objects of scientific and historical interest in the neighbourhood. The Trust also acts with other organisations, to facilitate community projects related to the enhancement of the Slate Islands.

The Slate Islands Heritage Centre at Ellenabeich, Isle of Seil, is open daily from April to October. The exhibition contains photographs, models and artifacts relating to the history, natural science and economics of the Slate Islands from the nineteenth to the twenty first century. Guides and Heritage Trails around the district are available.

The Easdale Island Museum is open daily from April to October. This award winning museum, now in its twenty first year, depicts the history of the Slate Industry, the life and times of the residents of Easdale and the geology and natural history of the island, recorded in photographs and artifacts.

Concession tickets are available which include access to both the Museum and the Heritage Centre and the five minute ferry crossing to Easdale Island.

Further enquiries to:
The Hon. Secretary,
Slate Islands Heritage Trust, Easdale Island, Argyll PA34 4TB

Bibliography

Netherlorn and its Neighbourhood, P H Gillies (Virtue, London, 1909)

Clans of the Scottish Highlands, R R McIan (Webb & Bower, Exeter, 1980)

Geology of Easdale Island, Laycock (unpublished manuscript c 1985 available Easdale Island Museum)

'The Slate Quarries of Easdale', D G Tucker, *Journal of Post Medieval Archaeology Vol 10* (Society of Post Medieval Archaeology, Oxford, 1976)

'The Island of Easdale', J Whyte, 3 articles *The Mining Journal Vols 34 & 35* (Railway & Commercial Gazette, London, 1861)

Western Isles of Scotland, Martin Martin (1716, republished by Birlinn, Edinburgh, 1994)

West Highland Steamers, Duckworth & Langmuir, (Stevenson & Sons, Prescot, Lancs, 1967)

The Clyde Puffer, Dan McDonald, (David & Charles, Newton Abbot, Devon, 1977)

The Royal Commission on the Ancient & Historical Monuments of Scotland, Argyll Vol.2, Lorn (HMSO, Edinburgh, 1974)

Highland Folk Ways, I F Grant, (Routledge & Kegan Paul, London, 1961)

Oban Times (extracts from 1880-1999 editions)

Statistical Reports of 1791 to 1891 (HM Government, available from Scottish Records Office, Edinburgh)

Writings, verbal reports and photographs of the slate quarriers of Belnahua, Easdale, Seil and Luing themselves, and their descendants.

Author's note:
The information given in this book is as accurate as historical research allows. Hearsay accounts have, wherever possible, been verified. Where this is not the case the text states clearly that the statement is supposition only.

Index

Some other books published by **LUATH** PRESS

Shale Voices

Alistair Findlay

foreword by Tam Dalyell MP

ISBN 0 946487 63 4 PBK £10.99

ISBN 0 946487 78 2 HBK £17.99

'He was at Addiewell oil works. Anyone goes in there is there for keeps.' JOE, Electrician

'There's shale from here to Ayr, you see.' DICK, a Drawer

'The way I describe it is, you're a coal miner and I'm a shale miner. You're a tramp and I'm a toff.'

HARRY, a Drawer

'There were sixteen or eighteen Simpsons...
...She was having one every dividend we would say.'
SISTERS, from Broxburn

Shale Voices offers a fascinating insight into shale mining, an industry that employed generations of Scots, had an impact on the social, political and cultural history of Scotland and gave birth to today's large oil companies. Author Alistair Findlay was born in the shale mining village of Winchburgh and is the fourth son of a shale miner, Bob Findlay, who became editor of the *West Lothian Courier*. *Shale Voices* combines oral history, local journalism and family history. The generations of communities involved in shale mining provide, in their own words, a unique documentation of the industry and its cultural and political impact.

Photographs, drawings, poetry and short stories make this a thought provoking and entertaining account. It is as much a joy to dip into and feast the eyes on as to read from cover to cover.

'Alistair Findlay has added a basic source material to the study of Scottish history that is invaluable and will be of great benefit to future generations. Scotland owes him a debt of gratitude for undertaking this work.'
TAM DALYELL MP

Tall Tales from an Island

Peter Macnab

ISBN 0 946487 07 3 PBK £8.99

Peter Macnab was born and reared on Mull. He heard many of these tales as a lad, and others he has listened to in later years.

There are humorous tales, grim tales, witty tales, tales of witchcraft, tales of love, tales of heroism, tales of treachery, historical tales and tales of yesteryear.

A popular lecturer, broadcaster and writer, Peter Macnab is the author of a number of books and articles about Mull, the island he knows so intimately and loves so much. As he himself puts it in his introduction to this book 'I am of the unswerving opinion that nowhere else in the world will you find a better way of life, nor a finer people with whom to share it.'

'All islands, it seems, have a rich store of characters whose stories represent a kind of sub-culture without which island life would be that much poorer. Macnab has succeeded in giving the retelling of the stories a special Mull flavour, so much so that one can visualise the storytellers sitting on a bench outside the house with a few cronies, puffing on their pipes and listening with nodding approval.'
WEST HIGHLAND FREE PRESS

Bare Feet and Tackety Boots

Archie Cameron

ISBN 0 946487 17 0 PBK £7.95

The island of Rum before the First World War was the playground of its rich absentee landowner. A survivor of life a century gone tells his story. Factors and schoolmasters, midges and poaching, deer, ducks and MacBrayne's steamers: here social history and personal anecdote create a record of a way of life gone not long ago but already almost forgotten. This is the story the gentry couldn't tell.

'This book is an important piece of social history, for it gives an insight into how the other half lived in an era the likes of which will never be seen again'
FORTHRIGHT MAGAZINE

'The authentic breath of the pawky, country-wise estate employee.' THE OBSERVER

'Well observed and detailed account of island life in the early years of this century'.
THE SCOTS MAGAZINE

'A very good read with the capacity to make the reader chuckle. A very talented writer.'
STORNOWAY GAZETTE

Crofting Years

Francis Thompson

ISBN 0 946487 06 5 PBK £6.95

Crofting is much more than a way of life. It is a storehouse of cultural, linguistic and moral values which holds together a scattered and struggling rural population. This book fills a blank in the written history of crofting over the last two centuries. Bloody conflicts and gunboat diplomacy, treachery, compassion, music and story: all figure in this mine of information on crofting in the Highlands and Islands of Scotland.

'I would recommend this book to all who are interested in the past, but even more so to those who are interested in the future survival of our way of life and culture'
STORNOWAY GAZETTE

'The book is a mine of information on many aspects of the past, among them the homes, the food, the music and the medicine of our crofting forebears.'
John M Macmillan, erstwhile
CROFTERS COMMISSIONER FOR LEWIS AND HARRIS

The Highland Geology Trail
John L Roberts
ISBN 0946487 36 7 PBK £4.99

Where can you find the oldest rocks in Europe?
Where can you see ancient hills around 800 million years old?
How do you tell whether a valley was carved out by a glacier, not a river?
What are the Fucoid Beds?
Where do you find rocks folded like putty?
How did great masses of rock pile up like snow in front of a snow-plough?
When did volcanoes spew lava and ash to form Skye, Mull and Rum?
Where can you find fossils on Skye?

'...a lucid introduction to the geological record in general, a jargon-free exposition of the regional background, and a series of descriptions of specific localities of geological interest on a 'trail' around the highlands.
Having checked out the local references on the ground, I can vouch for their accuracy and look forward to investigating farther afield, informed by this guide.
Great care has been taken to explain specific terms as they occur and, in so doing, John Roberts has created a resource of great value which is eminently usable by anyone with an interest in the outdoors...the best bargain you are likely to get as a geology book in the foreseeable future.'
Jim Johnston, PRESS AND JOURNAL

Rum: Nature's Island
Magnus Magnusson
ISBN 0 946487 32 4 £7.95 PBK

Rum: Nature's Island is the fascinating story of a Hebridean island from the earliest times through to the Clearances and its period as the sporting playground of a Lancashire industrial magnate, and on to its rebirth as a National Nature Reserve, a model for the active ecological management of Scotland's wild places.
Thoroughly researched and written in a lively accessible style, the book includes comprehensive coverage of the island's geology, animals and plants, and people, with a special chapter on the Edwardian extravaganza of Kinloch Castle. There is practical information for visitors to what was once known as 'the Forbidden Isle'; the book provides details of bothy and other accommodation, walks and nature trails. It closes with a positive vision for the island's future: biologically diverse, economically dynamic and ecologically sustainable.

Rum: Nature's Island is published in co-operation with Scottish Natural Heritage to mark the 40th anniversary of the acquisition of Rum by its predecessor, The Nature Conservancy

Tobermory Teuchter: a first-hand account of life on Mull in the early years of the 20th century
Peter Macnab
ISBN 0 946487 41 3 PBK £7.99

Peter Macnab was reared on Mull, as was his father, and his grandfather before him. In this book he provides a revealing account of life on Mull during the first quarter of the 20th century, focusing especially on the years of World War I. This enthralling social history of the island is set against Peter Macnab's early years as son of the governor of the Mull Poorhouse, one of the last in the Hebrides, and is illustrated throughout by photographs from his exceptional collection. Peter Macnab's 'fisherman's yarns' and other personal reminis-cences are told delightfully by a born storyteller.

This latest work from the author of a range of books about the island, including the standard study of Mull and Iona, reveals his unparalleled knowledge of and deep feeling for Mull and its people. After his long career with the Clydesdale Bank, first in Tobermory and later on the mainland, Peter, now 94, remains a teuchter at heart, proud of his island heritage.

'Peter Macnab is a man of words who doesnit mince his words - not where his beloved Mull is concerned. 'I will never forget some of the inmates of the poorhouse,' says Peter. 'Some of them were actually victims of the later Clearances. It was history at first hand, and there was no romance about it'. But Peter Macnab sees little creative point in crying over ancient injustices. For him the task is to help Mull in this century and beyond.'
SCOTS MAGAZINE May 1998

LUATH GUIDES TO SCOTLAND

These guides are not your traditional where-to-stay and what-to-eat books. They are companions in the rucksack or car seat, providing the discerning traveller with a blend of fiery opinion and moving description. Here you will find *'that curious pastiche of myths and legend and history that the Scots use to describe their heritage... what battle happened in which glen between which clans; where the Picts sacrificed bulls as recently as the 17th century... A lively counterpoint to the more standard, detached guidebook... Intriguing.'*

THE WASHINGTON POST

These are perfect guides for the discerning visitor or resident to keep close by for reading again and again, written by authors who invite you to share their intimate knowledge and love of the areas covered.

Mull and Iona: Highways and Byways

Peter Macnab

ISBN 0 946487 58 8 PBK £4.95

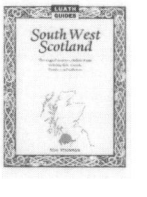

'The Isle of Mull is of Isles the fairest,
Of ocean's gems 'tis the first and rarest.'

So a local poet described it a hundred years ago, and this recently revised guide to Mull and sacred Iona, the most accessible islands of the Inner Hebrides, takes the reader on a delightful tour of these rare ocean gems, travelling with a native whose unparalleled knowledge and deep feeling for the area unlock the byways of the islands in all their natural beauty.

South West Scotland

Tom Atkinson

ISBN 0 946487 04 9 PBK £4.95

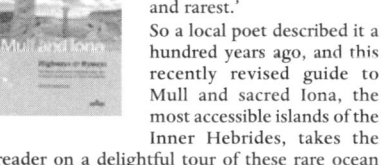

This descriptive guide to the magical country of Robert Burns covers Kyle, Carrick, Galloway, Dumfriesshire, Kirkcudbrightshire and Wigtownshire. Hills, unknown moors and unspoiled beaches grace a land steeped in history and legend and portrayed with affection and deep delight.

An essential book for the visitor who yearns to feel at home in this land of peace and grandeur.

The West Highlands: The Lonely Lands

Tom Atkinson

ISBN 0 946487 56 1 PBK £4.95

A guide to Inveraray, Glencoe, Loch Awe, Loch Lomond, Cowal, the Kyles of Bute and all of central Argyll written with insight, sympathy and loving detail. Once Atkinson has taken you there, these lands can never feel lonely. 'I have sought to make the complex simple, the beautiful accessible and the strange familiar,' he writes, and indeed he brings to the land a knowledge and affection only accessible to someone with intimate knowledge of the area.

A must for travellers and natives who want to delve beneath the surface.

'Highly personal and somewhat quirky... steeped in the lore of Scotland.'
THE WASHINGTON POST

The Northern Highlands: The Empty Lands

Tom Atkinson

ISBN 0 946487 55 3 PBK £4.95

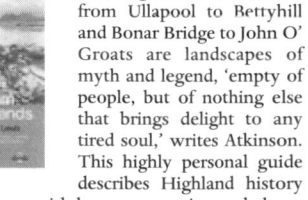

The Highlands of Scotland from Ullapool to Bettyhill and Bonar Bridge to John O' Groats are landscapes of myth and legend, 'empty of people, but of nothing else that brings delight to any tired soul,' writes Atkinson. This highly personal guide describes Highland history and landscape with love, compassion and above all sheer magic.

Essential reading for anyone who has dreamed of the Highlands.

The North West Highlands: Roads to the Isles

Tom Atkinson

ISBN 0 946487 54 5 PBK £4.95

Ardnamurchan, Morvern, Morar, Moidart and the west coast to Ullapool are included in this guide to the Far West and Far North of Scotland. An unspoiled land of mountains, lochs and silver sands is brought to the walker's toe-tips (and to the reader's fingertips) in this stark, serene and evocative account of town, country and legend. For any visitor to this Highland wonderland, Queen Victoria's favourite place on earth.

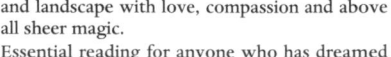

WALK WITH LUATH

Mountain Days & Bothy Nights

Dave Brown and Ian Mitchell

ISBN 0 946487 15 4 PBK £7.50

Acknowledged as a classic of mountain writing still in demand ten years after its first publication, this book takes you into the bothies, howffs and dosses on the Scottish hills. Fishgut Mac, Desperate Dan and Stumpy the Big Yin stalk hill and public house, evading gamekeepers and Royalty with a camaraderie which was the trademark of Scots hillwalking in the early days.

'The fun element comes through... how innocent the social polemic seems in our nastier world of today... the book for the rucksack this year.'
Hamish Brown,
SCOTTISH MOUNTAINEERING CLUB JOURNAL

The Joy of Hillwalking

Ralph Storer

ISBN 0 946487 28 6 PBK £7.50

Apart, perhaps, from the joy of sex, the joy of hillwalking brings more pleasure to more people than any other form of human activity.

'Alps, America, Scandinavia, you name it – Storer's been there, so why the hell should-n't he bring all these various and varied places into his observations... [He] even admits to losing his virginity after a day on the Aggy Ridge... Well worth its place alongside Storer's earlier works.' TAC

Scotland's Mountains before the Mountaineers

Ian R. Mitchell

ISBN 0 946487 39 1 PBK £9.99

In this ground-breaking book, Ian Mitchell tells the story of explorations and ascents in the Scottish Highlands in the days before mountaineering became a popular sport – when bandits, Jacobites, poachers and illicit distillers traditionally used the mountains as sanctuary. The book also gives a detailed account of the map makers, road builders, geologists, astronomers and naturalists, many of whom ascended hitherto untrodden summits while working in the Scottish Highlands.

Scotland's Mountains before the Mountaineers is divided into four Highland regions, with a map of each region showing key summits. While not designed primarily as a guide, it will be a useful handbook for walkers and climbers. Based on a wealth of new research, this book offers a fresh perspective that will fascinate climbers and mountaineers and everyone interested in the history of mountaineering, cartography, the evolution of landscape and the social history of the Scottish Highlands.

LUATH WALKING GUIDES

The highly respected and continually updated guides to the Cairngorms.

'Particularly good on local wildlife and how to see it' THE COUNTRYMAN

Walks in the Cairngorms

Ernest Cross

ISBN 0 946487 09 X PBK £4.95

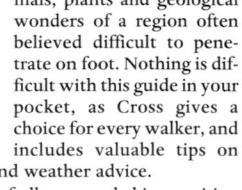

This selection of walks cele-brates the rare birds, ani-mals, plants and geological wonders of a region often believed difficult to pene-trate on foot. Nothing is dif-ficult with this guide in your pocket, as Cross gives a choice for every walker, and includes valuable tips on mountain safety and weather advice.
Ideal for walkers of all ages and skiers waiting for snowier skies.

Short Walks in the Cairngorms

Ernest Cross

ISBN 0 946487 23 5 PBK £4.95

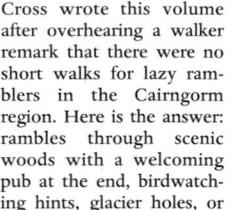

Cross wrote this volume after overhearing a walker remark that there were no short walks for lazy ram-blers in the Cairngorm region. Here is the answer: rambles through scenic woods with a welcoming pub at the end, birdwatch-ing hints, glacier holes, or for the fit and ambitious, scrambles up hills to admire vistas of glorious scenery. Wildlife in the Cairngorms is unequalled elsewhere in Britain, and here it is brought to the binoculars of any walker who treads quietly and with respect.

ON THE TRAIL OF

On the Trail of John Muir
Cherry Good
ISBN 0 946487 62 6 PBK £7.99

On the Trail of Mary Queen of Scots
J. Keith Cheetham
ISBN 0 946487 50 2 PBK £7.99

On the Trail of William Wallace
David R. Ross
ISBN 0 946487 47 2 PBK £7.99

On the Trail of Robert Burns
John Cairney
ISBN 0 946487 51 0 PBK £7.99

On the Trail of Bonnie Prince Charlie
David R. Ross
ISBN 0 946487 68 5 PBK £7.99

On the Trail of Queen Victoria in the Highlands
Ian R. Mitchell
ISBN 0 946487 79 0 PBK £7.99

On the Trail of Robert the Bruce
David R. Ross
ISBN 0 946487 52 9 PBK £7.99

On the Trail of Robert Service
GW Lockhart
ISBN 0 946487 24 3 PBK £7.99

On the Trail of the Pilgrim Fathers
J. Keith Cheetham
ISBN 0 946487 83 9 PBK £7.99

NEW SCOTLAND

Some Assembly Required: behind the scenes at the rebirth of the Scottish Parliament
David Shepherd
ISBN 0 946487 84 7 PBK £7.99

Scotland - Land and Power the agenda for land reform
Andy Wightman
ISBN 0 946487 70 7 PBK £5.00

Old Scotland New Scotland
Jeff Fallow
ISBN 0 946487 40 5 PBK £6.99

Notes from the North incorporating a brief history of the Scots and the English
Emma Wood
ISBN 0 946487 46 4 PBK £8.99

HISTORY

Reportage Scotland: History in the Making
Louise Yeoman
ISBN 0 946487 61 8 PBK £9.99

Blind Harry's Wallace
William Hamilton of Gilbertfield
introduced by Elspeth King
ISBN 0 946487 43 X HBK £15.00
ISBN 0 946487 33 2 PBK £8.99

Edinburgh's Historic Mile
Duncan Priddle
ISBN 0 946487 97 9 PBK £2.99

A Word for Scotland
Jack Campbell
foreword by Magnus Magnusson
ISBN 0 946487 48 0 PBK £12.99

BIOGRAPHY

The Last Lighthouse
Sharma Krauskopf
ISBN 0 946487 96 0 PBK £7.99

Come Dungeons Dark
John Taylor Caldwell
ISBN 0 946487 19 7 PBK £6.95

FOLKLORE

Scotland: Myth Legend & Folklore
Stuart McHardy
ISBN 0 946487 69 3 PBK £7.99

Luath Storyteller: Highland Myths & Legends
George W. Macpherson
ISBN 1 84282 003 6 PBK £5.00

The Supernatural Highlands
Francis Thompson
ISBN 0 946487 31 6 PBK £8.99

Tales from the North Coast
Alan Temperley
ISBN 0 946487 18 9 PBK £8.99

MUSIC AND DANCE

Highland Balls and Village Halls
GW Lockhart
ISBN 0 946487 12 X PBK £6.95

Fiddles & Folk: a celebration of the re-emergence of Scotland's musical heritage
GW Lockhart
ISBN 0 946487 38 3 PBK £7.95

FICTION

The Strange Case of R L Stevenson
Richard Woodhead
ISBN 0 946487 86 3 HBK £16.99

But n Ben A-Go-Go
Matthew Fitt
ISBN 0 946487 82 0 HBK £10.99

The Bannockburn Years
William Scott
ISBN 0 946487 34 0 PBK £7.95

The Great Melnikov
Hugh MacLachlan
ISBN 0 946487 42 1 PBK £7.95

POETRY

Poems to be read aloud
Collected and with an introduction by Tom Atkinson
ISBN 0 946487 00 6 PBK £5.00

Scots Poems to be Read Aloud
Collectit an wi an innin by
Stuart McHardy
ISBN 0 946487 81 2 PBK £5.00

Caledonian Cramboclink: verse, broadsheets and inconversation
William Neill
ISBN 0 946487 53 7 PBK £8.99

Men & Beasts
Valerie Gillies amd Rebecca Marr
ISBN 0 946487 92 8 PBK £15.00

The Luath Burns Companion
John Cairney
ISBN 1 84282 000 1 PBK £10.00

TRAVEL

Die kleine Schottlandfibel
Hans-Walter Arends
ISBN 0 946487 89 8 PBK £8.99

Edinburgh & Leith Pub Guide
Stuart McHardy
ISBN 0 946487 80 4 PBK £4.99

Pilgrims in the Rough: St Andrews beyond the 19th hole
Michael Tobert
ISBN 0 946487 74 X PBK £7.99

SPORT

Over the Top with the Tartan Army (Active Service 1992-97)
Andrew McArthur
ISBN 0 946487 45 6 PBK £7.99

Ski & Snowboard Scotland
Hilary Parke
ISBN 0 946487 35 9 PBK £6.99

Pilgrims in the Rough: St Andrews beyond the 19th hole
Michael Tobert
ISBN 0 946487 74 X PBK £7.99

CARTOONS

Broomie Law
Cinders McLeod
ISBN 0 946487 99 5 PBK £4.00

NATURAL SCOTLAND

Listen to the Trees
Don MacCaskill
ISBN 0 946487 65 0 PBK £9.99

Red Sky at Night
John Barrington
ISBN 0 946487 60 X PBK £8.99

Wild Scotland: the essential guide to finding the best of natural Scotland
James McCarthy
ISBN 0 946487 37 5 PBK £7.99

'Nothing But Heather!'
Gerry Cambridge
ISBN 0 94648749 9 PBK £15.00

Scotland, Land and People: An Inhabited Solitude:
James McCarthy
ISBN 0 946487 57 X PBK £7.99

Wild Lives: Otters – On the Swirl of the Tide
Bridget MacCaskill
ISBN 0 946487 67 7 PBK £9.99

Wild Lives: Foxes – The Blood is Wild
Bridget MacCaskill
ISBN 0 946487 71 5 PBK £9.99

Luath Press Limited
committed to publishing well written books worth reading

LUATH PRESS takes its name from Robert Burns, whose little collie Luath (*Gael.*, swift or nimble) tripped up Jean Armour at a wedding and gave him the chance to speak to the woman who was to be his wife and the abiding love of his life. Burns called one of *The Twa Dogs* Luath after Cuchullin's hunting dog in *Ossian's Fingal*. Luath Press grew up in the heart of Burns country, and now resides a few steps up the road from Burns' first lodgings in Edinburgh's Royal Mile.

Luath offers you distinctive writing with a hint of unexpected pleasures.

Most UK and US bookshops either carry our books in stock or can order them for you. To order direct from us, please send a £sterling cheque, postal order, international money order or your credit card details (number, address of cardholder and expiry date) to us at the address below. Please add post and packing as follows: UK – £1.00 per delivery address; overseas surface mail – £2.50 per delivery address; overseas airmail – £3.50 for the first book to each delivery address, plus £1.00 for each additional book by airmail to the same address. If your order is a gift, we will happily enclose your card or message at no extra charge.

Luath Press Limited
543/2 Castlehill
The Royal Mile
Edinburgh EH1 2ND
Scotland
Telephone: 0131 225 4326 (24 hours)
Fax: 0131 225 4324
email: gavin.macdougall@luath.co.uk
Website: www.luath.co.uk